The Motown Story

The Motown Story

ORBIS · LONDON

Acknowledgements
Photographs were supplied by Al Abrams, Cyrus
Andrews, Peter Benjaminson, Blues and Soul,
Adrian Boot, Rob Burt, CBS Records, Deluxe
Records, Robert Ellis, Charlie Gillett, Jazz Journal,
Peter Kanze, LFI, Wayne Léal, J P Leloir, Melody
Maker, Bill Millar, Motown Records, Michael Ochs,
Popperfoto, Pictorial Press, RCA Records, David
Redfern, Rex, Tom Sheehan, Star File, Syndication
International, Val Wilmer.

Editors
Ashley Brown
Michael Heatley

Executive Editor
Adrian Gilbert

Production Editor
Annette Kennerley

Chief Sub-Editor
Tom Hibbert

Sub-Editors
Chris Schüler
Alastair Dougall

Picture Editors
Sarah Smith
Dave Kent
Jonathan Reed

Editorial Secretary
Clare Witherden

Departmental Assistant
Darren Crook

Editorial Director
Brian Innes

Production Co-ordinator
Peter Taylor-Medhurst

Art Editor
John Heritage

Designer
Wayne Léal

Consultant Editors
Charlie Gillett
Phil Hardy
Bill Millar
Peter Brookesmith

Volume Editors
Graham Fuller
Lorrie Mack

CONTENTS

Introduction

'Berry has always felt that he's never been really appreciated', Diana Ross told 47 million people not too long ago. She was speaking during the closing minutes of the 'Motown 25: Yesterday, Today, Forever' television special, broadcast in the US in 1983 to celebrate Motown Records' 25th anniversary.

It's difficult to believe that Berry Gordy Jr., the man who founded and built the largest black-owned business in America, would feel that way. Yet it is in character, it is part of the same personality which, more than a quarter-century ago, drove him to pursue his ambitions with all the tenacity of a five-star general. It cannot be coincidental that Berry used to have a life-size portrait of himself posing as Napoleon, in full imperial garb, on a wall in his Detroit mansion. Bonaparte used to feel under-appreciated, too.

Motown's statistics these past 25 years are as impressive as those of any Napoleonic campaign. The company's artists have been among the most successful of the rock era. Measured by Top Ten hits on the US pop charts, for example, Stevie Wonder's total of 23 to date is exceeded only by that of Elvis Presley (38) and the Beatles (33). The Supremes collected 20 during their 'Hitsville USA' heyday, Marvin Gaye 17, the Temptations 15 and Diana Ross 11. These and other Motown performers have accumulated 150 Top Ten pop hits in America since 1960 (including 50 number ones) and almost 100 in Britain – to say nothing of numerous big-selling albums.

Sharing in the statistical triumphs are such writers and producers as Eddie and Brian Holland, Lamont Dozier and Norman Whitfield. They are among the American music industry's most accomplished hitmakers, Holland, Dozier and Holland having created more than 30 Top Ten entries, Whitfield more than 20. And Motown's Jobete Music division has published more major US hits than any other company in the rock era.

But the importance and influence of Berry Gordy's enterprise can't be measured merely by numbers. The man himself coined the phrase 'It's what's in the grooves that counts' for inscription into the logo of one of the company's subsidiary labels . . . and nobody said it better. The real measure of Motown's achievements is the music, from 'Money (That's What I Want)' to 'The Crown', from 'Shop Around' to 'All Night Long', from 'Please Mr Postman' to 'Cold Blooded'. This book tells the story of that music, from Detroit beginnings to international popularity, and of all the people involved.

'During the sixties', Marvin Gaye mused a couple of years ago, 'there was a struggle for black music acceptance among whites. Before Berry Gordy, it was thought of as not particularly chic to have black record collections in your home if you were white. Motown did a great deal to alleviate that.'

Closer to home and a few years earlier, British author Simon Frith suggested the same point, noting that Motown made soul music an essential sound in white pop. 'Previously there had been one-off soul successes', he wrote, 'selling on their *unique* appeal. After 1964, soul was a normal strand in pop music, a genre that white teenagers (British as well as American) *expected* to hear on the radio and the dance floor.'

Looking back to '64 and beyond to gain an understanding of Motown is not without hazards, especially if one's glasses are rose-coloured by silver anniversary celebrations. But the fact is that the company was innovative and influential, musically and culturally, in ways that are complex to chronicle.

Along with Phil Spector, Berry Gordy displayed a passion for 'quality control' that makes even some of today's high-tech producers look like amateurs by comparison. In the sixties, that passion was almost unprecedented in the creation of pop music.

Today, every major record company in the world boasts a department devoted to artist development. Twenty years ago, Motown's 'kick, turn, smile' (as the artists themselves called it) school was an innovation in helping young, gifted and black talent learn about their craft and come to terms with stardom.

Today, the American music industry has become infatuated with the power of television (by way of video music) to sell records. Way back when, Berry Gordy knew that his artists would secure and sustain popularity if they were regularly seen on the small screen by the widest possible (white) audience, and he took every opportunity that came along – first with appearances on 'The Ed Sullivan Show' (where the Supremes were almost fixtures) and, later, via Motown's own TV specials such as 'TCB' (Taking Care of Business) and 'Goin' Back To Indiana'.

These and other successful 'Hitsville USA' strategies – and some failures – are documented in depth in the following pages, along with assorted anecdotes: how, for example, an ice-covered highway caused a car carrying Berry Gordy, Smokey Robinson and several hundred first-run pressings of Motown's premier release to skid in front of a heavy truck, almost terminating Motown Records before it started. Or how cold beer and sandwiches in the wee small hours of the morning helped Holland/Dozier/Holland create their classic hits for the Four Tops and others. Or how teenage Stevie Wonder would torment his Motown tutors by deliberately walking into cars, missing staircase steps and frightening fellow airplane passengers with references to Judgment Day whenever turbulence struck.

This is the human side of Motown, in contrast to the image the company once purveyed of a highly-tuned machine turning out hit records as efficiently as Detroit's factories turned out automobiles. In fact, the latter public relations ploys probably said as much about Berry Gordy as Diana Ross' remarks on the 'Motown 25' TV special.

Gordy has been an intensely private man, and in the sixties as his company grew and prospered, he disappeared further and further into the background – even as Motown's press handouts and artist interviews became as bland and information-less as any in the music industry.

Likewise, the firm never allowed the limelight to shine on the heroes of the backroom: the musicians whose soul, talent and teamwork was at the heart of 'the Sound of Young America', and whose influence is everywhere in the music of the eighties.

This book is designed to illuminate some of those backrooms, among other aspects of Motown, and perhaps to help Berry Gordy realise that there are millions of music lovers in the world who appreciate only too well what he founded 25 years ago.

ADAM WHITE

The Making of Motown

The 'official' story of the rags to riches rise of Motown reads like a fairytale, but beneath Motown's phenomenal success lay sound business judgement, artistic flair and not a little heartbreak. The founder and director of the company, Berry Gordy, earned the respect of the music industry and of the business world, but he also came under criticism for his strong paternalistic control.

MOTOWN MAGICIAN

Berry Gordy put Detroit on the musical map

Until recently little was known of Berry Gordy Jnr's background. Such information as was available made no sense at all except on a romantic level, and Motown's official version of its own origins is curiously blunt. The aggressive young car-worker is said to have started the company that revolutionised the record industry on nothing more than an 800 dollar loan from his family's credit union. But this rags-to-riches account overlooks two factors. In the first instance, Gordy was among the hottest songwriters of the late Fifties and had several million-selling compositions to his credit. Moreover, he came – to borrow a phrase from Peter Benjaminson's *The Story Of Motown* – from a family as middle-class and as upwardly mobile as it was possible to be.

Berry Gordy Jnr was born on 28 November 1929 in Detroit, where he grew up in a Lower West Side household with four sisters and three brothers. Gordy Snr, a farmer from Georgia, had moved to Detroit some seven years earlier. He and his wife, Bertha, an insurance executive, eventually came to own a plastering business, a grocery store and a print-shop. By 1948, a black magazine had named them Family of the Year. Certainly, Gordy Jnr had no lack of proper schooling in either family unity or business administration; his parents, he has said, were the greatest producers he ever knew.

After a period as a professional featherweight in the late Forties (when he met fellow-boxer Jackie Wilson), Gordy was drafted for service in the Korean War in 1951. Discharged in 1953, he married 19-year-old Thelma Coleman, borrowed 700 dollars from his father and opened a record shop in Detroit. A self-confessed jazz buff, Gordy stocked the records of

Charlie Parker, Sonny Stitt and Art Tatum. 'People kept coming in asking for the Dominoes and Johnny Ace', he recalled. 'I couldn't understand it.' Reluctantly, Berry began to stock R&B records but too late to save his 3-D Record Mart, which went bankrupt. 'But I discovered that I really liked R&B, my feelings were not with jazz but with what I heard in the churches. I had to have that funky beat.'

Gordy next opted for what turned out to be a dull and unsatisfying job as a chrome trimmer on Ford's auto-assembly line. His marriage faltered and his wife filed for a divorce, which was eventually granted in 1959; despite Gordy's denials, the judge found him guilty of extreme and repeated cruelty.

Gordy began writing songs to offset the monotony of factory work. He pitched them to performers at Detroit's Flame Showbar – where two of his sisters had obtained the concession to sell cigarettes – and to R&B label-owners including the Bihari brothers, who ran Modern Records, and Don Robey of Duke and Peacock. 'I enjoyed writing blues. They had quite a few blues artists there and when I wrote a blues I'd send it to them.'

These companies, which often reaped extra royalties by adding fictitious names to the songwriting credits, did little to increase Gordy's fortunes. Nonetheless, in 1957 Berry left Ford and began collaborating with his sister, Gwendolyn Gordy, and Billy Davis, a distant relation who wrote under the pseudonym of Tyran Carlo. The trio succeeded in placing their songs with a publishing company whose owners managed Jackie Wilson.

One of the greatest soul singers, Wilson had left the Dominoes for a solo career on the Brunswick label. Gordy and Davis were asked to attend his recording sessions in New York under the supervision of orchestra leader Dick Jacobs. 'Reet Petite', their first song for Wilson, failed to dent the US Top Fifty in 1957 but made an enormous impact in Britain, where it went to Number 6. Novelty rock 'n'roll, it was not so much a coherent statement as a series of exclamations about a girl who filled her clothes from head to toe. High-pitched and ecstatic, Wilson simply let rip on it.

As well as rock'n'roll songs, Gordy was much taken with the kind of lushly orchestrated material that companies like Decca reserved for their stars of stage and screen. Wilson's version of 'To Be Loved' (1958), covered in Britain by Malcolm Vaughan, reached Number 22 in *Billboard*'s Hot Hundred and paved the way for a succession of operatic ballads with strings, monologues and huge, sobbing crescendos. Although such tissue-wrapped corn – 'Each Time', 'We Have Love' and others – lacked the finesse of the best of Tin Pan Alley, it was adored by middle-class black listeners.

Motown places and faces – label boss Berry Gordy (opposite above), the company HQ in Detroit (left) and early hitmakers Marv Johnson (opposite below left) and Smokey Robinson (opposite below right). Below 'We Are Family' – Mrs Gordy Sr (second right) and daughters Gwen (second left, with husband Harvey Fuqua), Anna (third left, with husband Marvin Gaye) and Loucye (right).

Above: Advertising for two hot Motown acts of the early Sixties. Below left: The inimitable Supremes, with Diana Ross (right). Below right: Mary Wells, who hit with Smokey Robinson's 'My Guy'.

Setting up in business

Gordy claimed not to have prospered from Wilson's successes: 'You can go broke with hits if someone else is producing them,' he said. His next step was obvious. Like Sam Phillips before him, Gordy bought a tape machine and began producing acetates for anyone who paid him 100 dollars. He and his wife-to-be, Raynoma Liles, rented studio time, hired professional musicians and began to recruit talented vocalists including the Miracles.

Anyone who could write 'Reet Petite' *and* 'To Be Loved' clearly had talent and it was to Berry Gordy that the Miracles' lead singer, Smokey Robinson, first turned for advice. 'He'd say "Well you left off this or didn't complete your idea on that,"' Robin-

son recalled. 'It really started me to think about songs and what they were. Gordy! Man, that cat more than anyone else helped me to get my things together.' Gordy leased the first Miracles tapes, including 'Got A Job' and '(I Need Some) Money', to the New York label, End. These titles reflected the faster doo-wop styles of the era, but they didn't sell and Gordy received no more than a one dollar ninety-eight royalty cheque.

Smokey Robinson claims to have urged Gordy to manufacture his own records and, in January 1959, Gordy inaugurated the Tamla label, setting up shop in a small clapboard villa on West Grand Boulevard. He called it Hitsville USA and hung a sign across the front of the two-storey building. Few of Detroit's small independent companies had ever bothered with the white audience and the primitive, dusty, backroom sound of Fortune or Sensation records rarely made the pop charts. But Marv Johnson's 'Come To Me' (Tamla 101)

changed the fiercely black, down-at-heel ambience of Fifties R&B into something light and frothy that sounded perfect on a transistor radio. Leased to United Artists, the record notched the Top Thirty in April 1959. Eddie Holland's 'Merry-Go-Round' (Tamla 102) went nowhere but Johnson, who was signed to United Artists, cranked out no fewer than nine consecutive hits.

All produced and co-written by Gordy, they represented the first rumblings of a distinctive Detroit soul sound. Girls bop-shoo-bopped in a thin, reedy fashion while a bassman hummed the kind of 'bottom' at which instrumentalists like Carol Kaye and James Jamerson would later excel. More importantly, someone was usually thumping a tambourine. 'I've always liked a lot of tambourine in our records,' said Gordy. 'I just happen to like the sound and I felt they added a very commercial feeling.' Gordy helped that tambourine-driven gospel sound – then unfamiliar to whites – to cross ethnic barriers.

Songs in the charts

'You Got What It Takes' and 'I Love The Way You Love' hit the Top Ten for Marv Johnson at the turn of the decade. The former, credited to the Gordys and Billy Davis (although Detroit bluesman Bobby Parker claims to have written it) would not look out of place among a sheaf of Smokey Robinson lyrics and the melody had the unhurried, instantly hummable and seductive quality of many later Motown classics.

Johnson remained in the charts throughout 1960. 'Ain't Gonna Be That Way' preceded 'Move Two Mountains', one of Gordy's few entirely self-composed songs and arguably his best. Incomparably catchy, it was covered in Britain by the Mudlarks. 'Merry-Go-Round' was the last of Johnson's early hits, but he resurfaced with 'I'll Pick A Rose For My Rose' in 1968.

Gordy and his wife – the Rayber Voices who provided the vocal accompaniment to

> 'He heard it all … he knew what a hit record was. Before Motown, he and my cousin, Billy Davis, wrote "Lonely Teardrops", "Reet Petite", all those records for Jackie Wilson … they knew where the music was, they put it together.'
>
> **Lawrence Payton** of the Four Tops on Berry Gordy

many of the first Tamla productions – expanded their roster throughout 1959. Like the Miracles, most of the performers came from street-corner groups who idolised Fortune Records' premier attraction, Nolan Strong and the Diablos. Records by Ron and Bill (Ronald White and Smokey Robinson), Nick and the Jaguars, the Fidelitones, the Swingin' Tigers and the Satintones made little impression, although the last-named spawned Robert Bateman, who co-wrote many of the Marvelettes' hits and introduced Gordy to Mary Wells. Eventually, the Miracles' 'Bad Girl' (Motown 1), which was leased to Chess, crept into the Hot Hundred in October 1959. It was the forerunner of Robinson's many fervent and mellifluous lead vocals.

The following month, Gordy produced 'Money' by Barrett Strong. The record was distributed by Anna, a label owned by Gwendolyn Gordy but named, in fact, after another of the sisters. The song, written by Berry Gordy and Janie Bradford (though John Lee Hooker has claimed authorship), combined a pounding gospel beat with brutally frank sentiments: 'Money, That's What I Want'. Berry was advised that disc jockeys wouldn't play a record that asked for cash at the height of the payola scandal but he ignored the warning and 'Money' reached Number 2 on the R&B chart in January 1960. Gordy's songs continued to be successful for other artists; 'Everyone Was There' had reached Number 96 for Bob Kayli in 1958 and 'All I Could Do Was Cry' (Number 33 in 1960) launched the most fruitful phase of Etta James' career.

Apart from 'Money', Gordy had relied on established, white-owned companies to distribute his records. They paid little or nothing in advance and, as long as they did the counting, very little in the way of royalties. In 1960, after 18 months of leasing his productions to larger labels, Gordy decided that Tamla should go national with the Miracles' 'Way Over There'.

'We're not making any money now,' Smokey Robinson had told him. 'We can't make any less by going national.'

Released on 9 July, 'Way Over There' was promoted with half-page advertisements in the US trade papers and the prophetic copy bears repeating: 'From out of the Mid West comes a new label destined to take its place among the leaders of the industry; Tamla, prexied by one of the young, driving geniuses of the music business today: Berry Gordy Jnr., Mr Hitsville.' Within a year or two this extravagant blurb was more than justified.

'Way Over There' sold 60,000 copies in three months. 'Now,' said Gordy in 1968, 'a figure like that would put us out of business. But then it was great because we had no overheads and we got many more distributors.'

Gordy Snr closed the family businesses and worked as Tamla-Motown's maintenance man; Gordy's sisters, Loucye and Esther, became chief administrators. Gwendolyn closed Anna Records, married Harvey Fuqua and set up the Tri-Phi and

Below: His master's voice – Berry Gordy at his desk. Bottom: Gordy Mansion, Detroit.

Harvey labels. Despite having a huge hit with the Spinners, their distributors refused to pay up and Fuqua joined Motown's Artist Development Department when Berry Gordy paid his debts. Apart from the Spinners and the Voice-Masters (whose line-up included such later giants as David Ruffin and Lamont Dozier) the acquisition of Tri-Phi brought Johnny Bristol, Shorty Long, Junior Walker and Ann Bogan of the Marvelettes into the Motown stable. By then, Ron White had discovered Stevie Wonder and Smokey Robinson had auditioned the Supremes.

Motown legacy

More and more artists flocked to Motown in the absence of any other successful Detroit independent. The Gordys and their in-laws – Marvin Gaye married Anna – were an increasingly powerful magnet to young and inexperienced black hopefuls who felt at ease within the small, family-oriented corporation. Within three years, using only local artists, Gordy had pushed gross sales of his company's records to more than four million dollars annually. He did so by giving his performers a sound, a style, an act and, above all, pride and prosperity.

In 1979 Gordy explained his success. 'We didn't have good enough equipment to make it sound like other companies so we had a different sound – but it was more of a freedom. Most of the writers and producers had no formal education but they had the choice of sitting in a studio creating something that would make them feel good and proud; or they could be robbing somebody's house or taking dope or doing any of the things people do when they don't feel the esteem they should feel. The people got caught up in this philosophy, this love for what they were doing and the freedom to create without going by rules and regulations. More important than the Motown sound, was the togetherness of the people.'   BILL MILLAR

Tamla Hits The Top

The irresistible rise of a black music company

BERRY GORDY had built Motown into a successful independent record label by 1962. But it was just one independent among others; one more record company that could prosper or go to the wall. The really spectacular rise of Motown came later in the Sixties when it flashed into the big league, outdistancing its small-time competitors and proving it could match the long-term financial success of the major corporations. That a black-owned business, promoting almost exclusively black acts, should achieve gross sales of 4.5 million dollars in 1963, a few years after Sun Records boss Sam Phillips had decided that black artists could never make it in the big league, was impressive. But it was astonishing that in 1977, the year that Phillips' 'white boy who sounded black' – Elvis Presley – died, Motown's gross earnings should total 61.4 million dollars. How did an ex-Ford production-line worker achieve this?

Quite simply, Berry Gordy had a strategy, a theory, of how to run a record company, and he imposed this on as talented a group of singers, musicians, producers and writers as has ever worked together in popular music. In the pursuit of this strategy, some careers were hamstrung or broken, some individuals ruthlessly ground down. Gordy often comes across as an ogre – seemingly megalomaniac in his obsessions and distasteful as a person. But for at least the 10 years from 1962, there was no doubting the quality of the music that came out – and this fact was immediately recognised in the market-place. In 1961, Motown had two Top Twenty hits in the USA. In 1962 it had six; in 1963 seven; in 1964 eleven; in 1965 nineteen and in 1966 twenty two. By then, the company was releasing, yearly, more hit singles than any other company.

Gordy's first rule was musical consistency, the application of what he called 'quality control'. Motown output was rigorously vetted, and the man who ran the company had complete faith in his own judgement. Other companies released a scatter of singles, hoping some would succeed, but Gordy only released records he was *sure* could make it. From 1960 to 1970, only 535 singles were put out – but 357, a proportion of over two-thirds, were hits. No other company could approach this percentage of chart successes.

On one level, this quality control involved the rejection of product that Gordy did not like; and the proportion of rejected tracks was high. At one meeting 68 recordings were discus-

Below: Berry Gordy Jnr, the former Ford chrome trimmer who brought the production line into music-making. The formula worked; by 1966, his Motown label was producing more hit singles per year than any other company.

sed, but only one was accepted. And Gordy did not change his methods as the company became more successful; he kept the new talent acquired on as tight a rein as he could, encouraging what often became cut-throat competition between artists, producers and songwriters to come up with one of the few tracks chosen for release. Sometimes three or four producers would be given the same song and be told to turn out the 'best' version.

Servants of the company

This atmosphere of competition and rivalry could easily turn to jealousy and infighting. But Gordy maintained a unified company through his determination to mould everyone to the corporate identity. Sometimes this took on a ludicrous aspect – the 'company song' which he insisted be sung before meetings, or official melon-eating contests, for example – but a combination of incentives and fear encouraged loyalty. The Motown 'house band' who played on the backing tracks were always well paid, and had to sign exclusive contracts to Motown. And gifts would be handed out for services rendered – Earl Van Dyke, who managed a Supremes tour, was given a 10,000-dollar bonus afterwards. Many individuals found this paternal system crushing, but Gordy had no qualms; for him, Tamla came first.

The final element of the Motown strategy was the tight financial and organisational structure. Berry Gordy undoubtedly made a fortune out of the company; but he refused to set up a spread of separate companies merely for tax-avoidance purposes. He preferred to keep as much of his operations as possible under his immediate control. To this end, also, he employed executives for their efficiency alone; by 1970, four out of the eight vice-presidents were white, and these men were experienced administrators rather than frustrated record producers or ambitious young men who might pose a threat. For Gordy needed to tighten his control as the company expanded and bought up some of its smaller rivals. Had he not done so, the strains that his idiosyncratic methods induced could have torn Motown apart. But within this strict corporate structure, he could maintain his position without fear of restraint. And the music produced was astounding.

ASHLEY BROWN

The New Generation

The growing pains of Berry Gordy enterprises

The array of Motown stars in a typical Sixties package tour. Left to right: The Temptations (in gold), Stevie Wonder (in blue), Smokey Robinson and the Miracles (in red), the Supremes (in black) and Martha and the Vandellas (in pink).

ALTHOUGH the Motown Corporation's position as a hugely successful independent record label and premier black American company remained fairly constant throughout the late Sixties and early Seventies, its nature altered considerably as a result of internal and external factors. Its influence on the music made by others gradually waned and, contrary to the end strived for by Berry Gordy in the Sixties, the lesson Motown learned in the following decade was that no label is a law unto itself. Now Motown followed more often than it led.

The disintegration of the company's 'family' image had begun in 1968 when the crucial creative partnership of Brian and Eddie Holland and Lamont Dozier departed, amid a flurry of litigation, to form their own Invictus and Hot Wax labels. And the tight control Gordy wielded over his artists was gradually loosening as they became aware of the increased freedom – and higher royalty payments – afforded to white rock acts.

At the same time, he began to lose interest in the day to day recording side of the label as he started looking for other entertainment markets in which to expand. Of these, the film world appeared most attractive. Recognising the potential movie star appeal of Diana Ross, lead singer of the Supremes, Gordy began to groom her for a solo career, billing the group as Diana Ross and the Supremes and then, in 1969, announcing her departure from the trio.

Golden wonder

With the help of Motown writers and producers Nick Ashford and Valerie Simpson, she was launched as a glossy performing celebrity via an extravagant TV special and one-woman shows on Broadway and in Las Vegas. Initially, she met critical derision – 'What's this?' scorned *Time* magazine. 'Diana Ross, ex-Supreme, making like Barbra Streisand?' – but her movie debut proved far more satisfactory and even gained her an Oscar nomination.

Gordy had timed his star's move into films wisely; Melvin Van Peebles' 1971 movie *Sweet Sweetback's Baadasssss Song* had triggered off a series of films with black stars – films such as *Shaft* and *Superfly* – and in 1973, Ross barged aside the competition to land the role of Billie Holiday in *Lady Sings The Blues*, a fine acting debut if a less than accurate portrait of the blues singer's music and life.

Meanwhile, on the records front, Gordy had moved his company, in 1971, from Detroit to Los Angeles, where both music and film industries were centred, and had founded new subsidiary labels in the rock-oriented Rare Earth and the broader-based MoWest.

The year 1971 proved to be critical for Motown in other respects, too: the contracts of most of Gordy's major artists came up for renewal, including that of Stevie Wonder, a star much coveted by other major labels. Wonder's immediate reaction on attaining majority was to demand all the money that had been held in trust for him (around a million dollars). In addition, he hired Johannen Vigoda, a New York lawyer skilled in contract negotiation, who wrested an unprecedentedly generous contract from Motown.

The new contract stipulated that Wonder would deliver completed tapes and cover artwork and Motown would press and distribute the product. The company retained virtually no artistic control. For a label once so autocratic in its handling of artists, this was little short of a complete *volte face*. But Motown *had* to keep Wonder for the obvious revenue he would generate and, perhaps just as important, for the prestige. Other artists, notably Marvin Gaye, also renegotiated their contracts, though none received such attractive terms as Wonder.

Motown matures

Both Wonder and Gaye immediately repaid Motown with splendid, influential LPs. Gaye's sensitive, socially aware work on *What's Going On*, in 1971, and its deeply sensual follow-up *Let's Get It On* ended a period of reassessment after the death of his duet partner, Tammi Terrell. *What's Going On* in particular gave Motown an important work to which it could point when answering criticisms of lack of concern about civil rights and the black political movements. Meanwhile, Stevie Wonder embarked on his sequence of mature LPs from *Where I'm Coming From* (1971) and *Music Of My Mind* (1972) through *Innervisions* (1973) to *Songs In The Key Of Life* (1976). It is arguable that no other pop songwriter produced such an irresistible body of work in the Seventies, and Wonder's 1972 US tour as guest of the Rolling Stones was the first step to gathering a significant white audience.

In fact, all of Motown's established stars coped well, initially, with the new decade's challenges. In a similar split to the Ross/Supremes schism, Smokey Robinson left the Miracles at the end of a marathon farewell tour; Norman Whitfield continued his development of the label's own psychedelic soul and large-palette orchestral soul with his productions for Undisputed Truth and the Temptations. The Supremes were quick to hit without Ross – 'Up The Ladder To The Roof' and 'Nathan Jones' both reaching the US Top Twenty in 1970 – and the Four Tops also maintained their chart success, while on the Soul subsidiary Gladys Knight and the Pips enjoyed their most productive spell.

Moreover, Motown had once again become the 'Sound of Young America' with the Jackson Five, a group of brothers from Gary, Indiana, fronted by the precocious and gifted singer Michael. Starting late in 1969 with 'I Want You

Right: Berry Gordy (left) with Diana Ross, the singer he groomed for superstardom. Below: The Jacksons took Motown into the Seventies, and then went on to attain greater fame elsewhere. Bottom: Three Motown superstars – Diana Ross and Marvin Gaye join Stevie Wonder (right) on stage at his 1980 Wembley concert. Both Gaye and Ross were soon to leave the Motown label, however.

Back', the Jackson Five bombarded the charts, outstripped the sales of the label's veterans, won Motown a new young audience and gave the label its first self-contained singing/playing band (albeit somewhat augmented at first).

But despite this continuing success it was clear that Motown was no longer making the influential musical moves. While it was market leader, established acts would put up with the cavalier treatment meted out to them. But when white rock labels came around waving cheque books and promising increased creative independence for the groups, they quickly left. The Four Tops, the Miracles, Gladys Knight and the Pips, the Temptations (since reunited with the label) and the Jackson Five (though brother Jermaine, who married one of Gordy's daughters, quit the group and stayed at Motown) were among the major artists in the gradual exodus; and producers Johnny Bristol, Norman Whitfield and Nick Ashford and Valerie Simpson also moved on.

The vacuum left by the departure of these acts and producers was never satisfactorily filled. Experienced artists newly-contracted to the label failed to receive the boost to their careers that they might once have expected, while the black music market was now moving to several different rhythms, none of them of Motown's making. Kenny Gamble and Leon Huff guided Philadelphia International into the premier spot with sophisticated orchestral ballads and dance sounds; in the deep south TK and its subsidiaries made lean and punchy disco hits; smaller regional labels such as All Platinum in New Jersey carved a slice of the dance market, while the European electronic-based disco sound was beginning to filter through.

Motown was slow to react to these mid-Seventies developments, continuing to rely on the old quartet of Wonder, Gaye, Ross and Robinson. But the label did unveil two major acts who at various times were the top draws in the black market. Both, however, made deals more akin to the Wonder and Gaye contracts than the straight production-line contracts offered to less obviously gifted new talents.

Commodores and competition
In the early Seventies Motown replaced the Jacksons with another self-contained band when they signed the Commodores, a group of college graduates from Tuskegee, Alabama, whose Lionel Richie became a gifted ballad composer. In the next decade Rick James, a singer/writer/producer/guitarist from Buffalo, finally came good with the excellent *Street Songs* album (1982).

Beside James and the Commodores, however, the rest of Motown's late Seventies signings and home-grown talent paled into embarrassing insignificance. The A&R department appears to have glanced at the charts at any one given time, noted a trend and signed the first band or soloist in that temporarily-popular mould; Grover Washington Jr and Ahmad Jamal joined briefly, for example, as a sop to the crossover jazz market. One form which continued to be successful for Motown, however, was the male-female duet as Gaye and Ross, Jerry Butler and Thelma Houston and Billy Preston and Syreeta carried on the tradition of Gaye's duets in the Sixties with Mary Wells, Kim Weston and Tammi Terrell.

But the impression of the late Seventies and early Eighties was one of a procession of faceless acts producing faceless music – acts such as Dr Strut, Nolen and Crossley, Switch, Apollo, Ozone, Flight, 21st Creation, High Inergy, Dazz Band, Tata Vega, Teena Marie, Kwick, Charlene and a distressingly longer list of even lesser-known groups.

Meanwhile, a decade after the mould-breaking contracts of Gaye and Wonder, the company finally lost two of its elder artists when Gaye moved to Columbia and, most surprisingly, Ross went to RCA (in the USA and Canada) and Capitol (elsewhere). It seemed that unless the label sharpened its acquisition of new talent, the once great pacemaker and tastemaker in black popular music would fall even further behind its competitors.
GEOFF BROWN

Hit Factory Formula

The secret of Motown's early success lay with Gordy's intuitive selection of talented artists. From this creative pool of musicians, singers, songwriters and producers came instantly memorable records of consistently lasting quality. Building on a strong foundation of professional acumen, plus the diverse skills of the Motown 'family' the company acquired a reputation for its fashionable yet sophicated image.

HITSVILLE USA

How Tamla mass-produced its chart entries

THE EARLY RECORDINGS on the Motown and Tamla labels lacked a distinctive unifying sound other than that of contemporary rhythm and blues, but as the market indicated its preference for certain types of Motown product, the company's core of songwriters and producers gained more self-confidence in their own personal sound and a house-style began to emerge. By 1962 those artists whose potential was proven, or was considered promising, started to receive the most attention while acts of questionable commercial viability were eased out. And around such talents as the Miracles, Mary Wells, Marvin Gaye, the Marvelettes, Little Stevie Wonder, the Temptations and the Supremes, Berry Gordy's creative team forged the unique Motown sound. The principal members of that team were Lamont Dozier and the Holland brothers, Brian and Eddie, who together were responsible for writing and producing a vast propor-

When the Supremes (overleaf) teamed up with writer-producers Lamont Dozier and Brian and Eddie Holland (below), Motown struck gold, for it proved to be a hugely successful alliance.

tion of Motown's output in the Sixties.

Eddie Holland had been born in Detroit on 30 October 1939. Having dropped out of college in the late Fifties, he went to work for Berry Gordy, singing demo discs of Gordy's songs for Jackie Wilson. A couple of Holland masters leased to United Artists in 1959 and 1960 went nowhere, but a year later he cut 'Jamie' for Motown itself and this reached Number 30 in the pop charts in January 1962.

The record was highly derivative of both Jackie Wilson's style and of the uptown R&B popularised by the Drifters but, significantly, it was the company's first product to feature the strings of the Detroit Symphony Orchestra (arranged by Gordy's second wife, Raynoma) which subsequently became a hallmark of the Motown sound. Later Holland sides were derivative too; these included 'If Cleopatra Took A Chance', which owed much to Smokey Robinson's productions for Mary Wells, and 'Baby Shake', which borrowed from Jackie Wilson's 'Baby Workout'.

By 1963, however, Holland was blueprinting the beginnings of a distinctive aural identity for himself and other artists, the result of a new and permanent songwriting and production partnership with his brother Brian and Lamont Dozier (born 16 June 1941 in Detroit). The elements of the sound they made their own were a bedrock bass-line; an emphatic beat accentuated by tambourines; pounding percussion and piano tracks; growling saxes; shrill female backup vocals in the classic call-and-response mode of gospel performances; and the swirling, riff-reinforcing strings of the Detroit Symphony.

During 1963, the new team worked with a number of Motown acts, including the Marvelettes ('Locking Up My Heart'), the Miracles ('Mickey's Monkey' and 'I Gotta Dance To Keep From Crying'), Martha and the Vandellas ('Come And Get These Memories' and 'Heat Wave'), Marvin Gaye ('Can I Get A Witness'), Mary Wells ('You Lost The Sweetest Boy') and the Supremes ('When The Lovelight Starts Shining Through His Eyes'). The records were far from identical – for one thing, the mix of the instrumental and vocal tracks varied – but they featured most elements, if not all, of the emerging sound and each one deservedly became a hit for Motown.

Eddie Holland's own recording of 'Leaving Here', a minor hit in 1964, also featured the basic blueprint, while his 'Candy To Me', issued several months later, was the improved model. All the previously-noted components were in place, and the infectious beat was emphasised by heavy handclaps and echo. The use of vibraphones added an arresting treble tone.

Supreme sandwich

The consummate exponents of Holland, Dozier and Holland's burgeoning creativity were the Supremes, for whom the team wrote and produced five consecutive Number 1 hits between July 1964 and the following May. The Supremes' first *Billboard* Number 1 came with 'Where Did Our Love Go', on which the song's melancholy was accentuated by a persistent piano motif; but as the sequence of hits continued, Holland, Dozier and Holland crafted a fuller, more metallic sound. (Singer Mary Wilson was unimpressed with the first draft of 'Where Did Our Love Go', and urged its creators to come up with less juvenile material.) Their habit of recording Diana Ross quickly on new material, before familiarity with a song smoothed out her vocal's rough edges, paid off time and time again, from the early successes right through to 'You Can't Hurry Love' and 'You Keep Me Hangin' On', a Number 1 hit towards the end of 1966.

The haste of the Supremes' recording sessions contrasts with the Holland-Dozier-Holland approach to the Four Tops, as group singer Levi Stubbs

recalled: 'We'd sit around and talk, and maybe sing a line at a time, and try to get a feeling for the tune; send out and get a sandwich or a cold beer, wait an hour 'til the sandwich settled, then we'd take another shot at it.'

Those remarks reach to the heart of Motown's creative process, and to the reasons for its success. Not only did the company have its own crew of songwriters and producers – it also had its own studio, operating 24 hours a day, seven days a week. Levi Stubbs remembered recording 'Baby I Need Your Loving' between two and eight o'clock in the morning, after Brian Holland told him about the song between drinks at the Twenty Grand night-club in Detroit.

In-house heroes

There were also in-house arrangers (among them, Maurice King, Hank Cosby, Ivy Hunter and Clarence Paul) and in-house engineers (headed by Michael McLain, who built and maintained much of the company's early recording equipment). There were in-house session singers (the Andantes and the Love-Tones) and, of course, there were the in-house musicians, the pulse of the Motown sound, its unsung heroes.

Leader of the house band was Earl Van Dyke, whose swirling organ underpinned hundreds of hits. Among his crew were guitarist Robert White, whose metallic, clanking sound encouraged the description of Motown records as production line pieces, factory noise set to music, and drummers Uriel Jones and Benny Benjamin, who provided the compulsive momentum of Holland, Dozier and Holland's best work, especially the rattling snares and distinctive tom-tom fills. James Jamerson's bass-lines anchored each rhythm track, lending depth and counterpointing the treble boost favoured by Gordy, while James Gitton's vibes

Below: Earl Van Dyke (front) and his quartet. In the Sixties, Van Dyke led the Motown house band, whose distinctive sound helped to forge the Motown style.

Brenda Holloway

BRENDA HOLLOWAY was born on 21 June 1946 in the small town of Atascadero, California, but by her teens was living in the ghetto district of Watts in Los Angeles and dreaming of showbusiness. Desperate for stardom, Brenda resorted to gatecrashing a convention in Los Angeles where she attracted the attention of Berry Gordy by singing along to the records of Mary Wells. A combination of vocal ability and svelte good looks secured her entry into Motown and she found herself commuting between Los Angeles and Detroit from 1962 onwards.

Her career on Tamla blossomed when she cut the anguished soul ballad 'Every Little Bit Hurts', which sold nearly a million copies and reached Number 13 in the Hot Hundred during May 1964. Slow and dramatic, ebbing and flowing with passion, it showcased her sinuous voice climbing over silky strings and the prominent piano of Lincoln Mayorga and was the first West Coast production to provide a sizeable hit for Motown. The song became a standard and was recorded by a wide range of singers including Stevie Winwood of the Spencer Davis Group (1965) and Southern songstress Peggy Scott (1970).

Equally intense symphonic soul followed with 'I'll Always Love You' (1964) before Brenda changed direction on the Smokey Robinson composition 'When I'm Gone', which reached Number 25 in April 1965. Here she employed the lighter phrasing of Mary Wells, who had originally recorded the song.

At this point Brenda Holloway, who possessed one of the richest voices in black music, was poised to become one of Detroit's leading singers. A run of highly attractive singles including 'Operator', 'Together Till The End Of Time', 'Hurt A Little Every Day' and 'Just Look What You've Done' culminated with her composition 'You've Made Me So Very Happy', released in

A sensuous voice and sultry good looks helped Brenda Holloway become one of Motown's top girls. Above: Relaxing with friends. Below: Pensive publicity.

late 1967. She envisaged this as a piece of vibrant psychedelia but was overruled by Berry Gordy, who insisted on a more seductive approach. Blood Sweat and Tears realised her true intentions and their rock version reached Number 2 in *Billboard*'s Hot Hundred in April 1969, selling two million copies.

By the late Sixties Brenda had become disillusioned with compromise, sharp practice and flesh peddling in the music business. She devoted herself instead to her family and her church. Later she charged Motown with falsely and fraudulently understating her royalties and won her case in 1972. During the Seventies she was involved in session work for a variety of artists including the San Remo Strings and Joe Cocker. Despite an attempt to revive her career on the Groove Merchant label in 1972, Brenda Holloway has since remained out of the public eye. CLIVE ANDERSON

Martha and the Vandellas

MARTHA REEVES was born on 18 July 1941 in Alabama, one of a family of 11 children raised as Methodists. She moved north to Detroit as a teenager and soon found favour singing classical repertoire on radio. Later she worked clubs in Toledo as Martha LaVelle, soul singer, and formed the Delphis with Rosalind Ashford and Annette Sterling. The group recorded for Checkmate without success, disbanded and then joined Motown, where Martha doubled as secretary and demo singer. With Rosalind and Annette she supported Marvin Gaye on 'Stubborn Kind Of Fellow' (1961) with such verve that they stole his thunder and, in the opinion of some, 'vandalised' his disc. As a result they were dubbed Martha and the Vandellas and signed to the Gordy label.

They made an auspicious debut in September 1962 with 'I'll Have To Let Him Go' and enjoyed success in the R&B listings with their second outing 'Come And Get These Memories' in April 1963. Their third disc, the Holland-Dozier-Holland composition 'Heat Wave', coupled with the mellifluous 'A Love Like Yours', peaked at Number 4 nationally in the summer of 1963, selling a million copies in the process. This release demonstrated Martha's ability to switch from hard-edged R&B to sultry soul ballads. 'Quicksand', issued in November, evinced exactly the same qualities as 'Heat Wave' and reached Number 8 in the Hot Hundred.

Annette departed in 1964 and was replaced by Betty Kelly. In August 1964 the Vandellas notched their second million-seller, the infectious 'Dancing In The Street', written by Marvin Gaye and William Stevenson; according to Martha it was conceived as an antidote to the inner city violence of the long hot summers. They were riding high and the hits followed fast, including 'Nowhere To Run' (1965), 'My Baby Loves Me' and 'I'm Ready For Love' (both 1966), 'Jimmy Mack' – a Hot Hundred Number 10 – and 'Love Bug Leave My Heart Alone' (both 1967). By November 1967 when they secured their final national hit, 'Honey Chile', they were billed as Martha Reeves and the Vandellas.

In 1968 Betty Kelly was replaced by Martha's younger sister, Lois Reeves from the Orlons, and the next year Rosalind Ashford gave way to Sandra Tilley of the Velvelettes. But despite attractive items like 'Honey Love' (1969) and 'In And Out Of My Life' (1971) the Vandellas were fading. Martha suffered a breakdown and by 1973 the group were finished. Lois joined Quiet Elegance on the Hi label and Martha went solo with MCA, where she worked on the *Willie Dynamite* soundtrack with J. J. Johnson, did session singing behind Ringo Starr, and recorded a peerless rock-soul set in *Martha Reeves* (1974).

Commercial success eluded her and so she moved to Arista, but neither her singles nor the album *The Rest Of My Life* (1976) made much impression. She later appeared as a TV actress but by the Eighties her career was in the doldrums.

CLIVE ANDERSON

Above and below: Images of Motown magic.

contributed to that treble mix with a ringing tone which also offset the percussive effect of tambourines. The final ingredient was supplied by Eddie (Bongo) Brown, whose conga work was especially important to the productions of Smokey Robinson and Norman Whitfield, lending them a fluid and supple quality which Holland, Dozier and Holland eschewed.

This rhythm section, augmented by dozens of other sidemen, was utilised in the studio in different ways. Some dates were recorded live, others with overdubs. Many backing tracks were not recorded in Detroit at all but were built on the foundations laid by Hollywood bass-player Carol Kaye and drummer Earl Palmer. These included the Supremes'

Martha Reeves (below left) and with the Vandellas (below).

'Back In My Arms', Marvin Gaye and Tammi Terrell's 'If I Could Build My Whole World Around You' and Stevie Wonder's 'I Was Made To Love Her'.

Since Motown's producers were also songwriters, they would frequently work first with the instrumental tracks, then the melody line, the lyric and the vocals. This process would often stimulate the artists, as Levi Stubbs pointed out: 'There would be an interaction with the songwriters. They would let you know what they were thinking about when they wrote the lyric and what mood they would like to create.' Then, he said, the Four Tops would offer their own interpretation based on that outline.

The Gordy approach

This informal and unstructured approach derived largely from Berry Gordy's own philosophy. 'I just always thought that

there were no rules,' he told a journalist on the occasion of Motown's 20th anniversary. 'If it sounded good, I thought it *was* good.' Another factor was the much-vaunted family atmosphere which prevailed within West Grand Boulevard during the early years.

Equally important to Gordy's philosophy was competition. Producers and songwriters vied with each other constantly for the right to record hot acts. Being responsible for one success didn't auto-

matically entitle them to the follow-up, although Holland, Dozier and Holland's franchise on the singles of the Supremes and the Four Tops was virtually exclusive between 1964 and 1967. Then there was quality control. The perpetual perfectionist, Gordy established this department under the auspices of Billie Jean Brown to screen every piece of product prior to release. For a long time, the Motown chief himself was the department, the final arbiter. He listened to everything, and was quick to send a recording back to its producer for remastering, remixing or more drastic surgery if it fell short of his expectations.

In fact, remixing was a constant occurrence, sometimes even after a record was released. Gordy knew that Motown's success depended on extensive radio exposure, particularly for the pop market, and producers were told to keep that in mind. No matter how impressive a record was when booming through large studio monitors, would it sound so good on the four-inch speakers of a car radio? Consequently, the company's singles were often mixed on small speakers atop the recording console, punching up the treble effect and utilising equalisation so that one or two instruments – the tight snare drum of Martha and the Vandellas' 'Nowhere To Run', for example, or the pounding bassline of the Supremes' 'You Can't Hurry Love' – jumped out of the AM airwaves within a record's first few seconds.

Uptight and husky

Another member of Gordy's creative team who contributed much to the development of the Motown sound was Norman Whitfield. He was first noticeable at Motown as author of a couple of early Temptations songs, and producer of Martha and the Vandellas' 'I'll Have To Let Him Go', but his 1964 work on the Velvelettes' 'Needle In A Haystack' and 'He Was Really Sayin' Something' demonstrated more dexterity with the Detroit sound.

In 1964, Whitfield accrued two Top Thirty hits – the Marvelettes' 'Too Many

The Marvelettes

ORIGINALLY the Marvelettes comprised Gladys Horton, Georgeanna Tillman, Katherine Anderson, Wanda Young and Juanita Cowart. All were born in Detroit in 1944. They were signed by Berry Gordy after winning a talent show at Inkster High School, where they were still in their senior year. Their first release on Tamla, 'Please Mr Postman', topped the national charts in the autumn of 1961 and went gold. A tour ensued and they became the first successful female group with Motown, paving the way for the Vandellas and the Supremes and doing much to establish the company.

Lead singer Gladys Horton possessed a distinctive, faintly adenoidal voice and the entire group exuded a fetching toughness. Along with Martha and the Vandellas they provided a welcome antidote to some of the more syrupy Motown effusions, especially after 1964 when the Supremes sighed their way to prominence. 'Please Mr Postman' inspired Dee Dee Sharp's 1962 smash hit 'Mashed Potato Time' and was successfully reworked by the Beatles in 1963 and the Carpenters in 1974. Especially effective was the 'Whoa yeah!' punctuation from the girls in unison, and most Marvelettes' sides benefited from such small touches. 'Playboy' (Number 7) was virtually a re-run of 'Postman' but the piano made a difference and there was a storming vocal finish. 'Beechwood 4-5789' (a US national Top Ten hit) had the girls rocking out their telephone number in a most seductive fashion in 1962 while 'Too Many Fish In The Sea', a Number 25 hit in late 1964, was lyrically neat and featured greasy sax embellishments.

The Marvelettes' material was supplied by such fine writers as Brian and Eddie Holland, Lamont Dozier, Norman Whitfield, Marvin Gaye, William Stevenson and Ivy Hunter, but some of their biggest successes came from the pen of Smokey Robinson. Prime examples include the superb admonition 'Don't Mess With Bill' (Number 7 in 1966), replete with rooting tenor sax, and 'The Hunter Gets Captured By The Game' (Number 13 in 1967). The latter song was covered in the Eighties by both Grace Jones and Blondie.

The line-up of the group changed frequently after 1963 when Juanita Cowart left. Georgeanna Tillman went next but the major blow came in 1968 with the departure of Gladys Horton. Ann Bogan (from the Andantes) was a competent replacement but times had changed and the hits were becoming more elusive. Only 'A Breathtaking Guy' (1970), another Smokey Robinson number, suggested their former glories. The Marvelettes broke up soon afterwards, but a re-formed line-up appeared in 1980. Both the group's past recordings and more recent interpretations of their material suggest that their legacy is far from exhausted.

CLIVE ANDERSON

The Marvelettes in the Sixties, when their career was at its peak.

Fish In The Sea' and the Temptations' 'Girl (Why You Wanna Make Me Blue)' – and, by mid 1966, he was the main man behind the Temptations, masterminding a tough and tense texture on their records in place of Smokey Robinson's alternately melancholy ('My Girl', 'Since I Lost My Baby') or exuberant ('My Baby', 'Get Ready') approach. In particular, the producer exploited David Ruffin's husky baritone and Eddie Kendricks' gossamer falsetto to good effect.

A further key exponent of Motown's mid-Sixties' sound was Mickey Stevenson. His work boasted no single identifying characteristic, but rather an endearing versatility. In 1963 and 1964 he handled Marvin Gaye ('Stubborn Kind Of Fellow', 'Hitch Hike', 'Pride And Joy') and the Marvelettes ('Beechwood 4-5789'). Then, as the Motown sound kicked into high gear, he proved equally comfortable producing numbers with a cutting edge (Martha and the Vandellas' 'Dancing In The Street', Junior Walker and the All Stars' 'Do The Boomerang', Stevie Wonder's 'Uptight') and ones with more orchestral leanings (Jimmy Ruffin's 'What Becomes Of The Brokenhearted', Martha and the Vandellas' 'My Baby Loves Me').

Stevenson was also notable for his productions with Kim Weston, among them 'Love Me All The Way', 'Just Loving You' and 'A Little More Love'. He also produced a couple of successful duets featuring Weston and Marvin Gaye, which neatly show the evolution of the Motown sound between 1964 and 1966. The first, 'What Good Am I Without You', is an infectious, midtempo outing, powered by percussion and bluesy piano work, in which Weston and Gaye trade lines. The second, 'It Takes Two', is an uptempo opus, with tambourines rather than handclaps emphasising the beat, and strings swirling around the couple's harmony vocals.

Mickey Stevenson shared his status as one of Motown's important second division producer-songwriters with a number of others: Hal Davis, Clarence Paul, Hank Cosby, Harvey Fuqua and Johnny Bristol. Davis and partner Marc Gordon, based in the company's Los Angeles office, were best known for their work with Brenda Holloway; Paul and Cosby worked mostly with Little Stevie Wonder (and were instrumental in harnessing and directing the youngster's extraordinary talents); and Fuqua and Bristol began collecting Motown credits in 1966 with Junior Walker and the All Stars, Gladys Knight and the Pips, and Marvin Gaye and Tammi Terrell.

Rats, roaches and talent

With so many producers, so many artists, it's little wonder that Motown's studio at 2648 West Grand Boulevard was in use all day, every day. Yet though record sales grew apace, the release rate of titles did not. In 1964, for example, the three primary labels (Tamla, Motown, Gordy) and two secondary outlets (Soul, VIP) put a total of 65 singles into national circulation. In 1966, the year of 'You Can't Hurry Love', 'Reach Out I'll Be There' and 15 other major hits, the company issued a mere 55.

The volume of singles released doesn't necessarily provide an accurate fix on the amount of recording done – Motown was issuing more albums in 1966 than in 1964 – but it does suggest basic stability. The company maintained its quality control procedures, too, although the old practice of inviting people off the street to hear and comment on new releases was phased out when certain producers began to deliver hits with unerring consistency.

But perhaps the moment when Berry Gordy finally felt he had achieved his goal of international recognition and acceptance for Motown's music and artists came in 1966 when, rather self-importantly, the company began to call itself 'The Sound of Young America'.

As a public relations exercise, this was undeniably more marketable – though considerably less convincing – than the phrase used by Gordy himself to describe his company's birth. The roots of Motown, he observed, were 'rats, roaches, talent, guts and love'. Nobody said it better.

ADAM WHITE

Left: Johnny Bristol started Junior Walker on his recording career and, as writer and producer, guided his recorded output. Below: Former premises of the Motown organisation in downtown Detroit.

MASTERPIECE

The production genius of Norman Whitfield

LEGEND CELEBRATES Holland-Dozier-Holland as the most successful architects of the Motown sound, and Smokey Robinson as the most gifted, but Norman Whitfield need stand in the shadow of neither reputation. Between 1966 and 1973, he produced 43 singles that reached *Billboard*'s Hot Hundred and included 19 Top Ten hits. For two years, 1969 and 1970, he was not only Motown's most successful producer, but also the most successful in the US. He was also the only producer to reach that nation's Top Ten with two versions of *two* of his hits: 'I Heard It Through The Grapevine' by Gladys Knight and the Pips (1967) and Marvin Gaye (1968), and '(I Know) I'm Losing You' by the Temptations (1966) and Rare Earth (1970).

Statistics aside, Whitfield was responsible for two of the most memorable soul records of the era – Gaye's 'Grapevine' and the Temptations' 'Papa Was A Rolling Stone' – and for introducing a progressive dimension to the music of the Motor City. During his heyday, he epitomised the producer's art, perpetuating the Phil Spector practice of using singers as musical instruments, as often interchangeable vehicles for his creative vision.

A growing reputation

His success wasn't instantaneous, however. Within Motown, Whitfield toiled in obscurity for years. A New Yorker whose family settled in Detroit by way of California, he joined Berry Gordy's fledgling enterprise in 1959 when he was 18. By 1963, Norman was accruing label credits on various Motown releases; he co-wrote Marvin Gaye's first Top Ten pop hit, 'Pride And Joy', and produced Kim Weston's 'It Should Have Been Me', an intense ballad which he later revived with both Gladys Knight and the Pips and Yvonne Fair.

Further recognition as a producer came in 1964 and 1965, through the Temptations' 'Girl (Why You Wanna Make Me Blue)', the Marvelettes' 'Too Many Fish In The Sea' and the Velvelettes' 'Needle In A Haystack'. Although all these hits were very much in the mainstream of the Motown sound, they also showcased their producer's affection for brash horn riffs and percussive rhythm tracks.

These preferences became more apparent when Whitfield took control of the Temptations' recording career in 1966, crafting a stunning series of hits – including 'Ain't Too Proud To Beg', 'Beauty Is Only Skin Deep', 'You're My Everything' and 'I Wish It Would Rain' – with emphasis on the group's most compelling component: the searing, soulful vocals of David Ruffin.

This swiftly elevated Whitfield's status within Motown, and he began producing several other acts, among them Jimmy Ruffin, Gladys Knight and the Pips, and Marvin Gaye. The records with Ruffin were much like those made with the Temptations, but sessions with Knight were more striking – especially 'I Heard It Through The Grapevine'.

The same song returned to the charts a year later, in the form of Whitfield's most innovative production. Marvin Gaye reportedly recorded 'Grapevine' before Knight, but it collected dust in Motown's tape library until material was needed for a new LP by the singer. The production was unlike anything Whitfield had recorded previously, or since; it was an arresting synthesis of musical ideas ancient (the voodoo drums, the rattlesnake tambourines) and modern (the metallic rhythm track, Gaye's menthol-cool vocal). The record exploded into the charts, then occupied the Number 1 position for seven weeks, selling four million copies in the US alone.

As a songwriter, Norman Whitfield's main asset was melody; lyrics came mostly from collaborators – Eddie Holland for a couple of years, then Barrett Strong. The latter partnership yielded 'I Wish It Would Rain' and 'I Heard It Through The Grapevine' among other hits, but really blossomed in the summer of 1968 when Whitfield wanted something special for the Temptations to compensate for David Ruffin's departure.

'Cloud Nine' was the result. For Motown, it was nothing short of revolutionary: psychedelic funk, propelled by wah-wah guitar, breakneck hi-hat and pistol-shot bass lines, with new lead singer Dennis Edwards and the other Temptations sharing vocal duties in the style of Sly and the Family Stone. Strong's lyrics were as bold as Whitfield's production: sharply-painted pictures of poverty, and of the singer's need to escape reality by way of 'cloud nine'.

Much more than the Supremes' 'Love Child', released only weeks before, the Temptations' record signalled Motown's recognition of its need to absorb and reflect the social and political changes of the late Sixties. Without that recognition, the Motown sound would soon have become irrelevant – music without a message.

So it was Whitfield and Strong who took Motown to the New Frontier, via the Temptations. For the next five years, the team tackled social commentary ('Runaway Child, Running Wild', 'Don't Let The Joneses Get You Down', 'Ball Of Confusion'), politics ('War', '1990', 'Ungena Za Ulimwengu'), racial issues ('Friendship Train', 'Message From A Black Man') and drugs ('Take A Look Around').

The music was electric, intense and highly rhythmic. Whitfield would select riffs, particularly those of guitarist Melvin Ragin, and expand, twist and elongate them throughout the texture of long instrumental tracks, embellished with brass, percussion, strings. Yet he could compress everything into a three-minute single with no less impact.

In addition to Ragin and arrangers Paul Riser, David Van DePitte and Jerry Long, the producer's studio crew included James Jamerson on bass, Earl Van Dyke on keyboards, Benny Benjamin or Uriel Jones on drums, Robert White on guitar, Jack Ashford on percussion and Eddie 'Bongo' Brown on congas and bongoes.

As for the Temptations themselves, Whitfield would write songs and lay down instrumental tracks while the group was touring, then have them add the vocals when they returned to Detroit. Despite this disjointed process, the results were seldom less than brilliant – and always commercial. The Temptations collected eight Top Ten pop hits in the post-'Cloud Nine' era, three of which made Number 1.

Star billing

Their commercial and aesthetic peak came in 1972 with 'Papa Was A Rolling Stone'. Whitfield once said of his early Seventies work, 'I wanted to try some songs that had the scope and feeling of a movie.' 'Papa' embodied that sonic widescreen approach, while displaying one of the most instantly recognisable introductions in popular music – that hypnotic bass line, the insistent hi-hat rhythm, those seductive string sweeps – and a great vocal hook.

The subsequent album, *Masterpiece*, with its 14-minute title track occupying most of one side, took the process a stage further; for many, it was a stage too far. It was not as well received as its predecessor and was generally considered 'overproduced', with too much Norman Whitfield and not enough Temptations.

The album was, however, a record of the status to which Whitfield had elevated the role of the producer; from an essential but anonymous backroom figure, he had become virtually a star in his own right, with his name on the front of the album cover and his portrait on the back.

Whitfield had also been working with Gladys Knight and the Pips, with whom he scored seven Top Ten R&B hits, and Edwin Starr, whose 'War' was a million-seller, but the Temptations remained his most effective vehicle. They were becoming increasingly impatient with the degree of control Whitfield exercised, however – especially as, after *Masterpiece*, he seemed to be failing to come up with hits. And, as they underwent personnel problems, Whitfield's attention wandered to a new group, the Undisputed Truth, with whom he had had a smash hit, 'Smiling Faces Sometimes', in 1971.

The Truth began to consume more of Whitfield's time, with increasingly erratic results – partly, perhaps, because he was no longer working with Barrett Strong. In 1974, the producer left Motown to form his own company, Whitfield Records. The roster included several ex-Motown acts: the Undisputed Truth, Willie Hutch and Junior Walker. But it was another of Whitfield's acts, Rose Royce, who were to be the most successful. Their 1976 soundtrack album for *Car Wash*, one of the first of the smash hit disco movies of the late Seventies, proved highly successful; composed and produced by Norman Whitfield, it showed him keeping abreast of musical fashion once again.

ADAM WHITE

Great Gordy Groups

Motown's 'kick, turn, smile' school of artist development ensured that every group emerged with a carefully-groomed image and an unmistakably Motown sound; one after another, The Four Tops, The Supremes, The Jackson Five and many more consolidated Motown's ascendancy. Even when the frenetic pace slowed, groups like The Commodores maintained Motown's position as the home of quality soul music.

T WIST 'N' FUNK

Four decades of Isley Brothers music

THE ISLEY BROTHERS have been one of the most durable of all black American acts. By adapting their style to changing trends in pop and rock they have registered hit records in four consecutive decades and have remained a top live attraction for almost a quarter of a century since 'Shout', their secularisation of frenzied gospel call-and-response singing, became their first Hot Hundred hit in 1959. The cornerstone of their success has been the lead voice of

Ronald Isley (born 21 May 1941), an unmistakeable tenor, sweet-toned but with a tough rasp and bite when pushed and a keen falsetto edge. His brothers Rudolph (born 1 April 1939) and O'Kelly (born 25 December 1937) lend vocal support to his lead.

The Isleys first lived in Cincinnati, Ohio, where their father, Kelly Sr and mother Sallye Bernice, sang and played organ in local Baptist churches. In 1944, when he was just three, Ronald won a 25-dollar war bond as first prize in a spiritual singing contest at the city's Union Baptist Church and, by the age of seven, he was appearing in larger shows with Dinah Washington, among others, at the city's Regal Theatre.

The family group toured churches in Ohio and Kentucky. A road crash in which one brother, Vernon, was killed almost persuaded the young brothers to give up but, encouraged to persevere by their mother, the Isleys quit Cincinnati in 1957 and took the Greyhound bus to New York. En route they met a lady named Bealah Bryant who had contacts in the big city's entertainment world and they were soon earning their keep singing in bars and clubs.

In 1957 the Isleys were signed to a small record label, Teenage, but the release of their first single, 'Angels Cried', was soured by the simultaneous death of their father. In 1958 they recorded for the Cindy and Gone labels, working on such graphic titles as 'Everybody's Gonna Rock'n'Roll' and 'Rockin' MacDonald'. Gone boss George Goldner re-issued the last title on Mark-X in the wake of the group's later successes.

In 1959 the brothers were signed to a major label, RCA, where their first single, 'I'm Gonna Knock On Your Door'/'Turn To

The Isley Brothers – twisting and shouting for a quarter of a century.

Me', did no better than the previous records, although the A-side provided hit material for Eddie Hodges in 1961. They had signed to the label because promotion man Howard Bloom saw them during a concert at Washington in 1959. Legend has it that one line in the Isleys' on-stage performance of Jackie Wilson's 'Lonely Teardrops' – 'You know you make me want to shout' – brought such a strong response from the audience that Bloom felt certain it could form the basis of a hit song on its own. He persuaded them to cut the disc at RCA's New York studios with producers Hugo and Luigi, using their Cincinnati home-town organist, Herman Stephens, on the session.

A simple, rousing gospel-based belter, 'Shout' made Number 47 in the *Billboard* Hot Hundred. Having set that tone, they followed up with a similarly impassioned performance on 'Respectable', but the record made no impact and other sides like 'Open Up Your Heart' and 'How Deep Is The Ocean' also failed. Both 'Shout' and 'Respectable' became popular songs for British beat groups to cover a few years later, as would other Isley songs of the early Sixties; 'Shout' itself made the US and UK Top Tens in the hands of Joey Dee and the Starlighters and Lulu and the Luvvers respectively.

Disappointed by the staid nature of RCA, dominated at the time by elderly executives, the Isleys moved on to Atlantic in December 1960. They cut four singles for the label, produced by Leiber and Stoller and mostly aimed at dance halls ('Teach Me How To Shimmy', 'Standing On The Dance Floor'), but enjoyed little commercial success. In 1962 they moved to Wand but their debut, 'Right Now', did no better. Their next single was a version of Bert Berns' 'Twist And Shout', originally recorded by the Top-Notes in 1961. One of the meaner Twist craze records, it catapulted the trio back into the charts in the summer of 1962 and was a Number 17 pop hit. The song again inspired covers, the Beatles' version being the most famous. The Isleys, however, couldn't capitalise with further hits – 'Twistin' With Linda' was a minor success but the superior 'Nobody But Me' flopped.

Destination Motown
The nomadic brothers moved on again, this time to United Artists in 1963, but had no luck there despite attempting a marriage of two styles ('Surf And Shout') and recording a first version of 'Who's That Lady', which was to be a Top Ten hit for them 10 years on as 'That Lady'. By 1964, they had moved to Teaneck, New Jersey, and formed their own label, T-Neck. Atlantic Records distributed their production of 'Testify Parts 1 and 2', on which Jimi Hendrix played guitar. Later singles, including 'The Last Girl', a fine soul performance, 'Simon Says', a souled-up version of the children's rhyme, and 'Move Over And Let Me Dance' appeared on the Atlantic label itself. None sold well, however.

Figuring they still had something to learn about business and production, the group went to the most successful black label of all time, Motown, in 1966. They were first teamed with producers Brian Holland and Lamont Dozier and set to work on a series of songs written by the producers with Eddie Holland. Released on the Tamla label, the Isleys' hits now became more regular, starting with 'This Old Heart Of Mine (Is Weak For You)', which made Number 12 in the US pop charts and, two years after its release, was a UK Number 3 in the winter of 1968. The Isleys had played in Britain just once, in October 1964, with the Searchers and Dionne Warwick. The 1968 hit was followed by three more British hits in 1969 – 'I Guess I'll Always Love You', 'Behind A Painted Smile' and 'Put Yourself In My Place'.

In the US 'This Old Heart Of Mine' was followed by a further minor hit in 'I Guess I'll Always Love You' (Number 61 in 1966), after which year Motown moved the group away from Holland and Dozier. Although they cut further singles on Tamla with other producers – 'Got To Have You Back' in 1967 with Ivy Hunter, for instance, and a reunion with Holland and Dozier in 1968 for 'Take Me In Your Arms (Rock Me A Little While)' – it was clear that the Isleys would never be allowed into the inner sanctum of long-established and influential personalities of Berry Gordy's tightly-knit company.

In an interview with *Rolling Stone* in 1978, O'Kelly said: 'Artists complained that we were getting too much good

Soul brothers: left to right Ronald, O'Kelly and Rudolph Isley. Together, they travelled the gospel road through Motor City to Seventies psychedelic funk.

3+3 equals success

The Isleys' own albums were selling well but not in the blockbuster volume of other top black acts. In 1973 they moved T-Neck's distribution from Buddah to CBS and had an immediate smash with 'That Lady', a US Top Ten pop hit and a Top Twenty UK hit taken from the *3+3* album. The LP successfully combined soul, rock, pop and funk influences to create a seamless whole. A reading of Seals and Crofts' 'Highways Of My Life' followed 'That Lady' into the UK charts, while other Top Twenty British hits of the Seventies were 'Summer Breeze', 'Harvest For The World' and 'It's A Disco Night'. To complement their new 'black pop' sound, the Isleys adopted the extravagant dress of post-Sly velvet and leather, denim and studs, suede and tassels – none of these clothes fastened above the waist.

Since *3+3*, the band's style and sound has grown in gradual, organic fashion, with Ernie's fluent, sustained-note solos as much a trademark as Ronald's singing. Since their version of Todd Rundgren's 'Hello It's Me' on 1974's *Live It Up* LP, the Isleys have written and produced all their own material. The 1977 LP *Go For Your Guns* with the powerful funk of 'The Pride', 'Tell Me When You Need It Again', 'Livin' In The Life' and ballads such as 'Voyage To Atlantis' and 'Footsteps In The Dark', is certainly one of the strongest albums of the Seventies and coincided with their move from Californian recording studios to Bearsville in New York, where they've worked ever since.

The Isley Brothers have established an enviable reputation, both as songwriters and performers, in rock. The Average White Band acknowledged their debt with a searing cover of 'Work To Do' on their second album and Rod Stewart took 'This Old Heart Of Mine' to Number 4 in the UK charts in 1975, while the Doobie Brothers' version of 'Take Me In Your Arms (Rock Me A Little While)', which made the US Top Twenty in the same year, repaid the Isleys' inclusion of 'Listen To The Music' on *3+3* two years earlier. Their single-minded approach to funk and ballads has made the long-lasting Isley Brothers a major black group, influential but rarely obviously imitated, so unique is their distinctive sound.

◄GEOFF BROWN

material; others complained that we were sounding like the Four Tops.' There's no doubt that the Isleys' version of 'It's Out Of The Question', a Smokey Robinson-Warren Moore song and production, *is* like a Four Tops cut, but considering that Motown had deliberately moulded the Contours earlier in the Sixties to sound like the Isleys the accusation of theft of another group's identity was far-fetched. Nevertheless, some at Tamla weren't displeased when the Isleys left the label in 1969 to reactivate their own T-Neck set-up, this time with distribution via Buddah.

New freedom, new mix

Their first release, 'It's Your Thing', was a Number 2 Hot Hundred hit in the spring of 1969. Lyrically it was much in tune with white rock of the day, to which the Isleys had been listening closely, but musically it was based on more traditional soul – the horn charts, for example, were pure Stax. In Britain, 'It's Your Thing' only reached Number 30, being overshadowed by the previously-mentioned Tamla recordings. However, the Isleys revelled in the freedom offered by their own label. They mixed quasi-political message songs ('Blackberries', 'Freedom') with earthy love songs ('I Turned You On', 'Was It Good To You') and achieved satisfying results.

Two other developments in the Isleys' pattern of work now became of lasting importance. They'd begun to use younger brothers Ernie and Marvin and Rudolph's brother-in-law Chris Jasper in the band.

Ernie, in particular, was a gifted musician who had started out on drums (making his live debut with them in 1966) but was inspired by José Feliciano to switch to acoustic rhythm guitar in 1968. He later played lead and was then clearly inspired by former Isleys' sideman Jimi Hendrix. Marvin was a good bassist, while Jasper's accomplished piano/organ work grew more central to the group's funk sound as electronic keyboards came to play a less melodic, more rhythmic role. During the week the youngsters studied music in college until the mid Seventies; weekends they were fully-fledged Isley Brothers.

The second major change was that from 1970 to 1974 the Isleys often covered white rock songs, a turnabout in the normal direction of cover versions. In 1971 their version of Stephen Stills' 'Love The One You're With' became their first major cross-over hit since 'It's Your Thing' when it reached Number 18 in the US pop charts. Dylan's 'Lay Lady Lay' and Carole King's 'It's Too Late' were also hits for the band, and they did a storming segued version of Hendrix's 'Machine Gun' and Neil Young's 'Ohio'. Most of the hits of this period were compiled in 1978 to form the aptly-titled *Timeless* album.

The group also tried to expand their T-Neck roster, signing Dave 'Baby' Cortez, Judy White, Marva Whitney and several others, but had no hits. They also financed their own film, *It's Your Thing* (1970).

The Four Tops' quarter-century of quality soul

'STANDING In The Shadows Of Love', 'Reach Out I'll Be There', 'Baby I Need Your Loving' – like a sheaf of yellowing love letters, the greatest moments of the Four Tops' long career retain the ability to touch the emotions. Two decades after Motown's golden age, when the combination of writers-producers Holland, Dozier and Holland and the Four Tops produced music of energy and warmth, the group's recordings still offer an open invitation to the dance floor.

The fact that the Four Tops remain a chart act and a major force in music in the Eighties may be ascribed, in large part, to that rare virtue, loyalty. Unlike most of their contemporaries in the first great wave of Motown groups, the Tops' line-up has never changed. Similarly, there has been no star billing for lead vocalist Levi Stubbs, which might have presaged a solo career and a dilution of the group's hit formula. The Tops stand four-square, a team that stuck together. 'We still enjoy singing together,' said Levi Stubbs in 1982, 'but we're friends first.'

Gospel roots

Their apprenticeship began when, as the Four Aims, they made their stage debut in 1954 in the Detroit neighbourhood in which they were born and raised. Levi Stubbs, Abdul 'Duke' Fakir, Lawrence Payton and Renaldo 'Obie' Benson refined their performing technique through a mixture of graduation balls, garden parties, socials and talent contests before themselves graduating to the club circuit. The group made a healthy living by playing one-nighters from Canada to Las Vegas. Their developing style relied heavily on gospel: said Levi, 'We were raised in the church, that's all we ever knew.'

An important figure in the early days was Lawrence Payton's cousin, Billy Davis. Active in the Detroit music scene, he encouraged the group to go on the road and eventually helped them to a contract with Chess Records in 1956. The Four Aims – so-called because they were 'aiming for the top' – had by now become the Four Tops. Despite both this optimistic change of name and the Chess label's success with local blues artists, sales of the group's Chess release disappointed and they were not retained. Subsequent liaisons with the Red Top, Columbia and Riverside labels also proved fruitless, and it seemed that the group might never break out of the club circuit, on which they enjoyed continuing success.

At this point, Billy Davis again took a hand. As the pseudonymous Tyran Carlo, Davis had penned hits for the fast-rising Jackie Wilson whom Levi Stubbs had briefly partnered in the Royals some years before. Davis' co-writer, Berry Gordy, was in the process of expanding his small-scale Motown record company. After a word from Billy the group contacted Gordy, who signed them up. Their first (and tentative) recording, *Breaking Through,* appeared on Motown's Workshop label and was a jazz album in the vein of the Hi-Los. They were then brought down to earth by a year-long stint with Billy Eckstine's Revue: Gordy felt that there was still room for improvement. This experience provided the finishing touch to their stage education and was to place them well ahead of their less experienced labelmates, whose sudden success often found them unprepared for the glare of the spotlight.

'The perfect marriage'

On their return from the road, the Tops were rushed into the studio – not as star performers, but as backing vocalists for Motown's first hit recordings. As Lawrence Payton commented: 'For a couple of years, we sang on practically every Motown record that was put out – you name it, we were on it.' Nevertheless Berry Gordy had not forgotten the Tops, and they were chosen to work with the producer-songwriting team of Eddie and Brian Holland and Lamont Dozier, a relationship that Payton later described as 'the perfect marriage'.

Lamont Dozier had been a friend of the group from early days and his knowledge of the Tops' vocal abilities was a major factor in the choice of 'Baby I Need Your Loving' as their Motown label debut. The song set the pattern for so many subsequent smashes: a harmonised intro followed by Levi Stubbs' pleading tones, the harmonies chiming in again on the chorus with renewed effect. Released in the summer of 1964, 'Baby I Need Your Loving' peaked at Number 11 in *Billboard*'s Hot Hundred; it was their first hit.

Holland, Dozier and Holland had other commitments within the Motown organisation, notably with the Supremes, but they managed to produce three more records for the Four Tops in the next nine months. It was the third of these, 'I Can't Help Myself', which hit the top in mid 1965. Curiously, its mid-paced tempo, tambourines and lush orchestration was reminiscent in many ways of the Supremes, whose position as Motown's hottest act was then under threat. Unlike their rivals, however, the Tops made only occasional appearances in the UK charts: 'Baby I Need Your Loving' had lost out to a typical Merseybeat cover by the Fourmost and subsequent releases had also failed.

Stateside success continued unabated, however. 'It's The Same Old Song' hit Number 5 and 'Ain't That Love', a genuine Four Tops oldie and one of Columbia's previously unsuccessful releases, entered the Hot Hundred, if only for a solitary week. From then on, the chart entries became as predictable as the sounds were rewarding. Even the group's lesser hits, like Stevie Wonder's 'Loving

The Four Tops in the Eighties – reaching out to success (below), a few years and several hits further on from their 1968 publicity shot (inset right). Insets far righ Levi Stubbs, lead singer with the Tops, woos the audience (above) while the group congregate around Brian Epstein (below)

h Out!

You Is Sweeter Than Ever', were subsequently covered by artists from Alan Price to Elton John. But the UK breakthrough was not to come until late 1966, with what was possibly the Tops' – and Holland-Dozier-Holland's – finest record.

From the haunting flute-and-oboe intro over an insistent drumbeat through the tambourine-laden verse to the chorus harmonies, 'Reach Out I'll Be There' had class stamped right through it. It was a deserved Number 1 on both sides of the Atlantic and established Levi Stubbs as 'the voice of Motown' for UK fans. From that point onwards, the Four Tops' releases rarely failed to make the UK Top Twenty, and the group began a rewarding relationship with British audiences, touring regularly.

Recipe for success
The Four Tops and their producers had found a winning formula. Take a mid to uptempo backing track of typical Motown style, let the instrumentation fall away to highlight the emotive, desperate tones of Levi Stubbs tackling a lyric of heartbreak and desertion – then the hook, a tidal wave of sound, would engulf the listener with harmony as the backing continued relentlessly. A trio of splendid hits in 1967 – 'Standing In The Shadows Of Love', 'Bernadette', and 'Seven Rooms Of Gloom' – continued the Tops' Top Twenty touch, although 'Bernadette', a hymn of devotion

with an epic Motown bass-line, departed from the group's usual type of lyric.

As one of the first internationally-famous Motown acts, the Tops had the chance to test out their stage act in front of many different audiences. Not that it was to change much over the years. As the backing band brought their instrumental warm-up to a close, the group (in matching suits) would bound up to the mike and hit the opening note as one. The first signs of sweat would see jackets discarded: Stubbs might remove his mike from its stand and move into a ballad, ad-libbing soulfully as Obie, Duke and Lawrence crooned stage right. Then – bang! uptempo again with the twinkling feet and sure routines born of countless club and cabaret dates. Like each of their songs, the Tops would build their act to a series of crescendos before quitting the stage with much hand-shaking and smiles.

Despite the group's consistency in the charts, later Holland-Dozier-Holland productions occasionally varied the ingredients of the hit recipe, but only by a little at a time. 'If I Were A Carpenter', a UK Number 7 and US Number 20 in early 1968, combined a contemporary folk-pop number (written by Tim Hardin) with a harpsichord-style backing, but the vocal quartet put the Four Tops' stamp on an

Right and below: The Four Tops conjure up their magical vocal harmonies. The group's line-up was (below from left): Obie Benson, Abdul Fakir, Lawrence Payton and Levi Stubbs.

ambitiously 'clean' sound. Albums came at the rate of two a year, but were for dedicated fans only, the obligatory brace of hit singles being accompanied by such unashamed fillers as the Monkees' 'Last Train To Clarksville'.

The departure from Motown of the Holland-Dozier-Holland team in 1968 was traumatic for the label as a whole; but the Four Tops eventually found an able replacement producer in Motown stalwart Frank Wilson, although the days of innovation were over. Unlike label-mates and contemporaries the Temptations, the Tops steered clear of psychedelia and social comment, restricting themselves to the emotion-filled numbers in which Stubbs' voice excelled. By the turn of the decade, however, the importance to the group of their former producers was evident from the Tops' decline to the lower reaches of the US Hot Hundred, although British fans remained comparatively loyal. Their recipe for success turned into a straitjacket.

Change in direction

The time was ripe for experiment, and one of the more interesting options taken up was a recording made with the Moody Blues in the early Seventies. The Tops had just come offstage after a one-nighter on a British tour when they were approached by Moodies' producer Tony Clarke with a demo of Mike Pinder's 'Simple Game' in hand. As Lawrence Payton remembers it, 'We didn't even know who he was. . . . We thought it was a good song, so the next day we went in, rehearsed and recorded it.' With the Moody Blues uncredited among the backing musicians and Payton sharing lead with Stubbs, the record was released in 1971 and made the UK Number 3 position. It was not merely nostalgic reasons that placed it at the end of the Four Tops' set on their 1982 UK tour a decade later.

The Tops rang the changes in the production sphere, too, with Ivy Hunter, Johnny Bristol and Smokey Robinson among those recruited – with varying success. It was widely felt that the group had passed their peak. Certainly, collaboration with the Diana-less Supremes yielded only insipid fare. An album released in 1972 showed both groups wearing cowboy gear and uncomfortable expressions on the cover; the record itself was hardly aural *Dynamite,* either.

The departure of the Four Tops from Motown shortly afterwards coincided with the company's move from Detroit to the West Coast. The label had embraced new sounds but the Tops had remained the same – and Motown no longer saw the group as a long-term money-spinner.

A parting of the ways was inevitable, but the choice of new label was surprising: Dunhill Records had made most of its money of out Sixties folk. The combination of the Tops and producers Brian Potter and Dennis Lambert achieved initial success with 'Keeper Of The Castle' – the title track of a popular album – and 'Ain't No Woman (Like The One I Got)', the only song of this period featured live in the Eighties; but this burst of popularity soon faded. The production team's subsequent success with Tavares in a similar field suggests that the group was unable to get out of the rut, but such projects as the soundtrack to *Shaft In Africa* (1974) seemed wholly ill-advised.

The group had clocked up nearly a quarter-century in the business, and the gruelling round of touring and recording was one from which they wanted to escape for domestic and professional reasons. Writers Obie Benson and Lawrence Payton took time out to write for Marvin Gaye and Aretha Franklin respectively; Benson co-wrote the influential 'What's Going On'. Live appearances, when they happened, tended to be cabaret seasons rather than the one-nighters that had formed the schedule in the Fifties and Sixties. It wasn't so much a case of selling out as going back to their roots in the Detroit days, even if it meant reliving former glories night after night.

During their exile from the charts, the Four Tops had watched and listened to the groups who were changing the face of black music. When they signed with Casablanca Records in 1980 it seemed as if they might have tied themselves to the disco bandwagon with a label best-known for promoting such acts as Donna Summer and Lipps Inc. But the Tops were taking positive steps to put the hitless years behind them. 'With disco, we found ourselves a little disoriented,' recalled Payton, 'but Casablanca wanted to go with a different thing.' The label paired them with producer David Wolfert and provided a nucleus of musicians previously known as sidemen for West Coast 'white-soul' artists. Accepting that they were no longer dictators of style, the Tops decided on a more sophisticated feel.

Released in late 1981, 'When She Was My Girl' deserved its success in the UK and US charts. Obie Benson's acappella bass was especially attractive and the use of a melodica as solo instrument was both unusual and effective. The follow-up, 'Don't Walk Away', boasted a 'popping' octave bass-line worthy of Earth, Wind and Fire, while the album *Tonight* (1982) bore witness to the fact that, whatever the musical changes, the Tops were still in fine and distinctive vocal form. And during their 27-date tour of the UK in 1982 the group showed a renewed relish for live performance. The sound they produced was undeniably of the Sixties, yet it continues to exert a strong appeal despite the many vagaries of fashion.

MICHAEL HEATLEY

Four Tops
Recommended Listening

The Best Of The Four Tops (K-Tel NE 1160) (Includes: Reach Out I'll Be There, Walk Away Renee, Standing In The Shadows Of Love, Seven Rooms Of Gloom, If I Were A Carpenter, Bernadette, You Keep Running Away). *Greatest Hits 1972–1976* (MCA MCL 1675) (Includes: Ain't No Woman, Are You Man Enough, Catfish, One Chain Don't Make A Prison, Keeper Of The Castle, Sweet Understanding Love). *Tonight* (Phonogram 6480 058) (Includes: When She Was My Girl, From A Distance, Tonight I'm Gonna Love You All Over, Don't Walk Away).

The Four Tops relax, away from the tension and glitter of the stage.

GLADYS KNIGHT AND THE PIPS

Soul veterans
who struck gold

WITH A CAREER spanning some three decades, Gladys Knight and the Pips can justifiably claim to have achieved every goal that popular music has to offer. They have won Grammy Awards, received gold and platinum discs by the score, appeared on virtually every stage around the world, performed for royalty and heads of state – yet they have continued to perform and record, their enthusiasm undiminished.

First Knights

Gladys (born 28 May 1944) began singing almost as soon as she could talk. She joined the choir of her local church and her natural talent prompted her mother to put Gladys's name on the list of competitors on the radio show 'Ted Mack's Amateur Hour' by the time she was eight. Gladys won three heats before walking off with the first prize of 2000 dollars at Madison Square Garden for her rendition of 'Too Young'. After spending a year on the road with Ted Mack, Gladys headed home to Atlanta, Georgia.

A birthday celebration for Gladys's elder brother Merald led to an impromptu singing session with Gladys, Merald, sister Brenda and cousins William and Elenor Guest. The family group kept together, rehearsing during the week and performing together at church, with two more cousins involved – Edward Patten as singer and James Wood as manager. James's nickname was 'Pip', and when the question of a group name came up it was he who suggested the Pips.

The Pips made their first record in 1957 for Brunswick, 'Whistle My Love', which failed to sell and led to both Brenda and Elenor leaving the group. By 1961, however, the remaining Pips had secured a residency at the Builders' Club in Atlanta. After a show one night, the owner, Clifford Hunter, asked the Pips to try out some primitive recording equipment he had recently purchased. One of the songs the group performed, Johnny Otis's 'Every Beat Of My Heart', sounded good enough to release as a single. Hunter and his partner Tommy Brown set up the Huntom label, and put out 'Every Beat Of My Heart' to good local reaction.

Bobby Robinson, owner of the Fire and Fury labels based in New York, heard about the single and sent word down to Atlanta that if the Pips were prepared to come to New York he would record them. The Pips sold whatever personal items they had to raise the fare and, on arriving in New York, went into the studio to re-cut 'Every Beat Of My Heart' with 'Room In My Heart' as the flipside. However, after a further two singles for Fury things began to go wrong for the Pips. Langston George, who had joined the Pips in 1957, departed – as did Gladys herself, in order to start a family. The three remaining Pips continued to record for a while, making a

couple of singles for Fire/Fury before the company folded.

It was with some relief for all concerned that Gladys decided to rejoin the group towards the end of 1963, and a new recording deal with Maxx Records, founded by Larry Maxwell, soon followed. He put them in the hands of Van McCoy, who produced a hit first time out with 'Giving Up'. The success that the Maxx single achieved prompted both Vee-Jay and Bobby Robinson's new label Enjoy to delve into their back catalogues for material by the group. Yet after a couple of further hits, and with barely a year of their Maxx contract expired, Larry Maxwell went bankrupt; Gladys Knight and the Pips were out in the cold again. Fortunately, thanks to the Pips' growing reputation for live performance, it wasn't long before Motown Records signed them.

In the clear

In retrospect, it has to be said that their Motown stay promised much but delivered little. Only rarely were the Pips given the best material with which to work. They started off working with Norman Whitfield, who gave them hits in 1967 with 'Take Me In Your Arms And Love Me', 'Everybody Needs Love' and 'I Heard It Through The Grapevine', which made Number 2 in the US.

However, writer/producer Whitfield's policy of milking every song for all it was worth quickly saw Marvin Gaye hit Number 1 on both sides of the Atlantic with the same song. In later years, whenever the Pips performed it they would be unfairly slated for covering 'Marvin's song'. Another number that was originally a hit in 1968 for the Pips was 'It Should Have Been Me'; the song became an even more successful record for Yvonne Fair some eight years later.

Gladys Knight and the Pips: from the Motown shadows (above) to the Seventies spotlight (top and opposite).

Despite having further hit singles, Gladys Knight and the Pips were keen to leave Motown. In March 1972 they signed to Buddah, ironically while they were at the Number 1 spot in the US with 'Neither One Of Us'. Jim Weatherly, the composer of that song, became as sought-after as Gladys Knight and the Pips, and Buddah were quick to secure his signature as well. This decision was to pay dividends – further Weatherly numbers such as 'Best Thing That Ever Happened To Me' and 'Midnight Train To Georgia' became international hits. In addition, the Pips were awarded two Grammys in 1973, one for the Best R&B Vocal Performance for 'Midnight Train To Georgia' and the other for the Best Pop Vocal Performance for 'Neither One Of Us'.

Buddah continued to keep Gladys Knight and the Pips in the forefront of soul music for some seven years, mainly by ensuring that they were given the best pro-ducers to work with. Van McCoy returned in 1977 to give them another international hit with 'Baby Don't Change Your Mind'; Curtis Mayfield worked with them on the soundtrack LP to the film *Claudine* (1974); Tony Camillo produced the hit 'Perfect Love', while Ralph Moss helped supply the group with their hit record 'Try To Remember – The Way We Were'.

Gladys Knight made her acting debut in *Pipe Dreams* (1976), while the Pips, having made their solo debut with 'Street Brother', finally recorded their own albums for Casablanca, *At Last . . . The Pips* and *Callin'* (both 1978). Gladys herself cut a solo album for Buddah, *Miss Gladys Knight* (1979), which prompted rumours of a rift in the family group. Those rumours were scotched a year later, however, when Gladys Knight and the Pips signed with CBS. Nickolas Ashford and Valerie Simpson, who produced many of the Pips' Motown sides, returned to give them further hits with 'Bourgie Bourgie' and 'Taste Of Bitter Love'.

In 1983, a new chapter appeared to be unfolding for the group. Leon Sylvers III, whose writing and production skills had brought both Shalamar and the Whispers to international prominence, completed an album with the Pips. Michael Jackson had also been mentioned as a possible producer for subsequent recordings, further securing Gladys Knight and the Pips' future in what was, remarkably, their fourth decade together.   GRAHAM BETTS

Gladys Knight and the Pips Recommended Listening

Spotlight On Gladys Knight And The Pips (Buddah SPOT 1006) (Includes: Midnight Train To Georgia, Part Time Love, Come Back And Finish What You Started, It's A Better Than Good Time, So Sad The Song).

The Supremes
MOTOWN

Glamour, grooming and the greatest songs

WHEN DIANA ROSS, Mary Wilson and Florence Ballard first began singing together in Detroit in the late Fifties, there were few female superstars in rock'n'roll or R&B. There were even fewer female groups of any consequence, perhaps only the Chantels. Yet this male supremacy didn't deter the three teenage schoolgirls from pursuing a career in music, nor ultimately prevent them from becoming one of the most successful acts in the history of rock.

The Supremes accumulated more Number 1 hits (12) in the US than anyone except Elvis Presley and the Beatles. They reached the Top Ten 19 times between 1964 and 1969, and generated record sales estimated to exceed 50 million. The group *defined* the Motown sound of the Sixties – its innovation, its influence, its popularity. Their acceptance served to bridge the gap between pop and R&B and helped to make the music of black America more accessible to millions worldwide. Theirs was a triumph of style, too, for the Supremes' sophisticated image – the glamour and the grooming, the choreography and the coiffure – often seemed as important as the music itself.

Top right: Diana Ross (left) with fellow original Supremes Mary Wilson (centre) and Florence Ballard (right). Left and right: Performing before an evocative set on the 1965 Motown tour of Britain. Below: The Supremes confer with Lamont Dozier and Brian and Eddie Holland, writers and producers of many of the group's hits during the golden years of the mid Sixties.

Getting out of the ghetto

The Supremes' evolution from ghetto kids to international celebrities is a crowded and convoluted story. Two of the three principals were born in Detroit, Diana Ross on 26 March 1944 and Florence Ballard on 30 June 1943; Mary Wilson (born 6 March 1944) came from Greenville, Mississippi, but grew up in the Motor City. Wilson and Ballard attended Northeastern Junior High School and met after their performances in a talent contest. They formed a group with a third girl, Betty Travis, and were encouraged in their endeavours by Paul Williams and Eddie Kendricks, part of an amateur act known as the Primes. The intention was for the girls to be the Primes' sister group, the Primettes, and Williams recruited Diana Ross from Cass Technical High School to bolster their vocal capabilities. When Travis left for personal reasons, Barbara Martin joined the line-up.

During 1959-60, the two groups performed in and around Detroit at parties, record hops and talent contests. The Primes then merged with another local group, the Distants, and subsequently became the Temptations. The Primettes secured work with Detroit-based LuPine Records, handling backing vocals for various artists, and recording their own disc debut, 'Pretty Baby'/'Tears Of Sorrow'. This LuPine release coupled uptempo material on both sides, but was poorly recorded.

The Detroit music community was anxious to see whether the creative skills Berry Gordy had demonstrated with Marv Johnson, Jackie Wilson and Smokey Robinson's Miracles could be sustained and developed. Diana Ross, who lived in Smokey Robinson's neighbourhood, sought to attract Gordy's attention with the Primettes. This led to an audition at Motown and their first contact with Gordy himself.

Pinpointing the group's chronology at this time is difficult, as there are many conflicting recollections (even when the Supremes were superstars, their Motown biographies were short on detail, long on public relations puffery). The most accepted version suggests that Gordy was interested in working with the girls only after they graduated from high school. This they did, the story goes, and returned to Motown to begin recording as backing singers, then as an act in their own right.

But since the group's first Motown record, 'I Want A Guy', was released in March 1961, before the girls graduated, it seems more likely that Gordy signed them immediately or soon after the audition, while requiring them to continue their education. Gordy is also said to have sought a new name for the group, and so Florence Ballard picked 'the Supremes' from a list compiled at short notice before contracts were signed.

Popcorn and blues

'I Want A Guy' was the first of six Supremes singles released between 1961 and 1963, at the rate of two a year. The other five were 'Buttered Popcorn', 'Your Heart Belongs To Me', 'Let Me Go The Right Way', 'You Bring Back Memories' and 'A Breathtaking Guy'. They featured a variety of R&B styles – no surprise, since Motown itself was then striving for its creative and commercial identity – and none sold outside Detroit until the company's staying power was proven to distributors through hits by the Miracles, the Marvelettes and Mary Wells.

Three of the six records were written and produced by Gordy. 'I Want A Guy' was a melancholy ballad notable for Ross's nasal lead and the use of the producer's favoured instrument, the flute; 'Buttered Popcorn' was a perky novelty item in the 'Mashed Potato' mould of the time, with Ross on lead again. 'Let Me Go The Right Way', a percussive, Latin-tinged number, saw Florence as featured vocalist. Smokey Robinson penned and produced the other three 45s, all featuring Ross on lead vocals. 'You Bring Back Memories' rocked along in the style of the Isley Brothers' 'Twist And Shout', while 'Your Heart Belongs To Me' and 'A Breathtaking Guy' reflected Robinson's increasingly popular productions with Mary Wells – subtle ballads with unobtrusive rhythm tracks and mellow harmonies.

The first two of these singles were issued on the Tamla label, after which the Supremes were permanently transferred to Motown. 'A Breathtaking Guy' sold the most copies, peaking one-quarter of the way up *Billboard*'s Hot Hundred in August 1963.

The Supremes also served as backing singers for a number of other Motown artists. The most celebrated sessions on which their voices can be heard include Mary Wells' 'You Lost The Sweetest Boy', Kim Weston's 'It Should Have Been Me' and Marvin Gaye's 'You're A Wonderful One'. At some undetermined point during these formative years, Barbara Martin left the quartet, although not before their first publicity photos were distributed in 1962.

The failure of Gordy and Robinson to produce a substantial hit for the Supremes by the autumn of 1963 must have been frustrating, particularly since another Motown girl group, the Marvelettes, had accumulated three Top Twenty hits by then, and yet another, Martha Reeves and the Vandellas, was riding *Billboard*'s Hot Hundred at Number 4 with 'Heat Wave'. So the Supremes began working with the writers and producers of the latter record, a trio whose individual talents were known within Motown, but whose combined strengths were only just becoming apparent: Eddie and Brian Holland and Lamont Dozier. The sessions paid off immediately with the first significant hit of the Supremes' career, 'When The Lovelight Starts Shining Through His Eyes'.

Cindy Birdsong (left) took over from Florence Ballard in 1967.

Where the Supremes' previous recordings lacked self-confidence, 'Lovelight' was bold and brash, with its Bo Diddley beat and beefy brass. Though the vocals were undermixed amid splashing cymbals and driving drums, the girls strutted their stuff with sufficient style to secure a Top Thirty chart entry by January 1964. A follow-up, 'Run Run Run', flopped, but Holland-Dozier-Holland had other material on hand.

It's been said that 'Where Did Our Love Go' would have been given to Mary Wells had she not chosen to leave Berry Gordy's enterprise in 1964. She was certainly the company's hottest artist that spring, with 'My Guy' at the top of the US charts. The Supremes were soon to replace Wells as the Motown favourites, however. 'Where Did Our Love Go' was recorded by the Supremes, and released in June. Its appeal was obvious, immediate, its ingredients irresistible: the footstomping introduction, the insistent piano riff, the emphatic beat, the ethereal echo of the backing harmonies ('baby, baby . . .') and, most of all, Diana Ross's aching, agonised lead vocal.

'Plenty of jump in this one', noted *Billboard*'s review of this 'rockin' blues groove'. Rockin' was right: within three weeks, the record was in the Top Twenty; by August, it was Number 1. For Ross, Wilson and Ballard, the good news reached them on the road, touring with Dick Clark's summer 'Caravan of Stars'. The Supremes had performed regularly with the Motortown Revue, but Berry Gordy was anxious to see them secure wider (white) recognition. Indifferent audience response at the beginning of Clark's tour changed to enthusiasm as 'Where Did Our Love Go' vaulted up the charts.

The next single solidified this success. 'Baby Love' contained the same components as its predecessor, but was punchier and more polished; the combination of Ross's inviting vocal and the unforgettable chorus was electric. 'Baby Love' was the epitome of the Motown sound, the R&B/pop fusion on which the company built its reputation, and proved its excellence by spending four weeks at Number 1 that November. Britain was equally captivated. 'Where Did Our Love Go' crushed a local cover version by Peter Jay and the Jaywalkers and reached the Top Three in October; 'Baby Love' climbed to Number 1 less than two months later.

Album outings

Motown, meanwhile, moved to capitalise upon the album sales potential of the Supremes bonanza. An LP entitled *Where Did Our Love Go* was issued in September 1964 and spawned the act's third consecutive US singles chart-topper, 'Come See About Me'. In November came *A Little Bit Of Liverpool*, featuring covers of such British originals as 'A Hard Day's Night', 'World Without Love', 'Bits And Pieces' and 'Can't Buy Me Love'. The following March there was the self-explanatory *Country, Western And Pop*.

These were of variable quality. While the Holland brothers and Lamont Dozier concentrated on the Supremes' singles, others handled the LP tasks during 1964-65: Clarence Paul, Lawrence Horn, Berry Gordy, Hal Davis, Marc Gordon and Harvey Fuqua were among those entrusted with album production duties. It was an understandable arrangement, however, given that Motown's creative and financial momentum was coming from the singles – of which the company sold 12 million in 1964. For their part, the Supremes earned 300,000 dollars that year, although Gordy exerted close control over their finances; Mary Wilson claimed that, even in 1974, she still needed Gordy's signature to enable her to withdraw personal savings from her bank in Beverly Hills.

The next 12 months saw the Supremes sustain their hot streak with three more Number 1 records in the US ('Stop In The Name Of Love', 'Back In My Arms Again', 'I Hear A Symphony') and only one com-

parative failure ('Nothing But Heart-
aches', which reached Number 11 in the
summer of 1965). Each new release became something of an industry event, as
Holland-Dozier-Holland progressively
evolved the group's sound.

'Stop In The Name Of Love' was especially bold, thanks to some of Eddie Holland's
better lyrics and a terrific rhythm track,
with swirling organ, ringing vibes, rattling tambourines and that perpetual, pro-
pulsive beat. The record augmented its
American chart credentials with three
weeks in the UK Top Ten, coinciding with
the Motortown Revue's sole excursion to
Europe, with the Supremes as headliners.

It was a busy time for the Motown dar-
lings – all tours and recording. Diana Ross
spent so little time at her Detroit home
that a visitor to the house swore the stove
had never been used. The group appeared
in a number of TV specials, and also in the
somewhat unlikely role of three nuns in
the 'Tarzan' series. Such was their popularity that, during a waterside concert in
Barbados in 1965 before a crowd of thou-
sands of males, the group had to escape by

*All that glitters . . . the
Supremes shone like stars in
their shimmering robes (above
and top right), but it was Ross
(right) who was singled out by
Berry Gordy for a solo career.*

boat when a number of over-
enthusiastic fans stormed the stage
and demanded the girl's glittering
gowns as souvenirs.

The same year, the group made
their debut at New York's Copa-
cabana night-club, fulfilling
Berry Gordy's desire to see his
artists travel beyond the confines
of the R&B and pop music markets
– to become accepted by America's
showbiz establishment, by the likes
of Sammy Davis Jr and Carol Chan-
ning, whom he would later ask to
write sleeve notes for Supremes LPs.
Billboard's review of that concert
must have been sweet music to
Gordy's ears. The Supremes 'will be
around a long time as a top adult act',
reported the publication. The girls

'can handle the old music hall song-and-dance bit' and have 'a sharp comic sense and a repertorial range worthy of a veteran group'.

It was this strategy that sparked the first significant criticism of Motown. Most fans were suspicious of the old-fashioned show-biz values Gordy was so anxious to embrace; to them, the music of the Motor City was young, honest and relevant in ways that the cabaret set could never understand. Not surprisingly, therefore, *The Supremes At The Copa* (1965), *The Supremes Sing Rodgers and Hart* (1967) and *The Supremes Sing And Perform 'Funny Girl'* (1968) were among the group's less popular albums.

The criticism and the poor record sales failed to change Gordy's plan, however. He emphatically wanted his performers to be all-round entertainers, as the early formation of Motown's artist development division – the 'kick, turn, smile' school – made only too clear. The young, poor and inexperienced girls who became the Supremes had been keen to comply with Gordy's demands. The lookalikes, in their sequinned gowns, were geared to appeal to a white middle-class audience; they did not wear their hair natural and allowed their name to be used to promote white bread in commercials.

Diana Ross appeared only too willing to become an all-round entertainer. This, after all, was the youngster who was named her school's 'best dressed girl', who designed clothes in her spare time, and who improved her mind reading bound volumes of *Classics Illustrated*. And Ross was hardly indifferent to Berry Gordy's wishes; for many years, the two were known to be intimate, even close to marriage. Gordy's ambition for Ross, and the continuous pressures of life on the road, in the studio, always in the spotlight, combined to produce serious internal problems for the Supremes in 1966-67. Florence Ballard was particularly unhappy.

Creative mix'n'match
In terms of record sales, this period was business as usual. The creativity of the Holland-Dozier-Holland team was at its peak, with 'My World Is Empty Without You' and 'Love Is Like An Itching In My Heart' (both US Top Ten entries), 'You Can't Hurry Love', 'You Keep Me Hangin' On' and 'Love Is Here And Now You're Gone' (all US Number 1 and UK Top Twenty hits) and three consecutive US Top Ten albums. The recording process was increasingly mix'n'match, mixing one lead vocal with another rhythm track waxed weeks apart and dubbing in background voices recorded at yet another time. But the results were still impressive. 'My World Is Empty Without You', 'You Keep Me Hangin' On' and 'Love Is Here And Now You're Gone' were remarkable productions, all tension and texture.

Tension was mounting within the group at this time, too, though accounts of the events surrounding Florence Ballard's de-

Above: Diana Ross comforts one of Florence Ballard's daughters at the former Supreme's funeral. Below: Preparing for a public appearance.

parture from the Supremes in the spring of 1967 differ widely. Some claim that Ballard began skipping rehearsals, recording sessions and even concert appearances. Others suggest she was a victim of Motown's ruthless image-conscious, star-moulding policy.

Ballard had weight problems and perhaps did not fit the slick Supremes line-up; she claimed she was ousted. The pressure may also have had not a little to do with Gordy's growing ambition to make Ross into a megastar. Ballard said that during her seven years as a Supreme, Motown gave her a small weekly allowance and she believed the rest was being invested for her. When she left Motown, she claimed she was given only a small lump sum. She sued Gordy, Ross and others for conspiring to push her out of the group, but failed.

After an unsuccessful attempt at a solo

career, Ballard's fortunes hit rock bottom when her husband left her, she was mugged and robbed and ended up on welfare with her three young daughters to support. Her tragic life ended in poverty in Detroit in February 1976 – one report says as a result of a heart attack brought on by taking weight-loss pills and alcohol. With Ballard gone – and perhaps to minimise publicity of her rumour-shrouded exit – Gordy seized the opportunity to push Ross upfront and grant her separate billing to emphasise her lead role.

Diana Ross and the Supremes became a showcase for Ross's talents and the renaming was also a device to pave the way for a future solo career. This procedure also took place with another Motown group – Smokey Robinson and the Miracles, originally simply the Miracles. Ballard's place was filled by Cindy Birdsong (born 15 December 1939), formerly of Patti LaBelle and the Bluebelles.

The first record to carry the new identity was 'Reflections', a US Number 2 and UK Number 5 that was followed by two relatively unsuccessful releases – 'In And Out Of Love' and 'Forever Came Today'. The problem was compounded by another behind-the-scenes wrangle at Motown, involving royalty disagreements between the company and Holland-Dozier-Holland, which led to the team leaving in a flurry of legal action. Motown was also faced with the competition from the then-popular trends of acid rock and psychedelia.

Yielding to Temptations
The emotive 'Love Child' restored the group to the Number 1 spot in the US in November 1968. It was a haunting song about desire in the slums, reflecting the developing awareness of conditions in the black ghettoes, though it was ironic that the song was in fact penned by one of the few whites in the Motown empire – Canadian-born R. Dean Taylor.

The decline was temporarily arrested, too, by the union of Diana Ross and the Supremes with the Temptations, yielding the hit single, 'I'm Gonna Make You Love Me' (a US Number 2 in early 1969), several hit albums and a couple of highly successful American TV specials. But the shows were thinly-disguised vehicles for Ross to demonstrate her talents as an all-round entertainer. She sang Broadway evergreens and Tin Pan Alley standards, performed carefully-choreographed dance routines, participated in comedy sketches and, for old times' sake, threw in a couple of Supremes hits.

Recording with the group seemed increasingly less important to Ross, and it showed on two singles, 'No Matter What Sign You Are' and 'The Composer'. Both failed to reach the Top Thirty on either side of the Atlantic. To the surprise of few, Diana Ross announced she was leaving the Supremes in October 1969. It was a risk for Motown to split the group, but also a gamble in that they could come out of the move with two top acts instead of one.

Motown released Ross's farewell single with the Supremes – 'Someday We'll Be Together' – a mournful ballad which might have been written for the occasion (but wasn't). The last record to top the US charts in the Sixties, it was an appropriate sign-off for one of America's most successful groups of the decade. The venue at which Ross made her final appearance with the Supremes on 14 January 1970 was the Frontier Hotel, Las Vegas; the showbiz audience was the antithesis of the record buyers who had elevated the group to superstardom in 1964, but aptly reflected Gordy's success in taking Diana Ross to a new and profitable public.

As for the Supremes, Motown recruited Chicago-born Jean Terrell, sister of boxer Ernie Terrell (with whom she briefly recorded) to replace Diana. She was a dynamic and distinctive stylist and for a couple of years the Supremes continued to collect hit records – especially in Britain, where 'Up The Ladder To The Roof', 'Stoned Love', 'Nathan Jones', 'Floy Joy', and 'Automatically Sunshine' all made the Top Ten in the period from 1970 to 1972; a sixth, 'River Deep, Mountain High' (with the Four Tops) made Number 11 in 1971.

After 1972, however, the quality of the trio's records became erratic, as did Motown's promotional commitment. Various producers, including Jimmy Webb, Stevie Wonder and Brian Holland failed to improve matters, which, in turn, were complicated by membership changes: Cindy Birdsong was replaced by Lynda Laurence, who later left along with Jean Terrell: they were replaced by Scherrie Payne and Susaye Green.

Founder member Mary Wilson sustained the group for a few more years in between a solo venture and litigation against Motown. Then she and the label finally laid the Supremes to rest, with 50-50 ownership which prevented either party resurrecting the name without the other's consent.

ADAM WHITE

THE SUPREMES
Discography

Singles
I Want A Guy/Never Again (Tamla 54038, 1961); Buttered Popcorn/Who's Loving You (Tamla 54045, 1961); Your Heart Belongs To Me/He's Seventeen (Motown 1027, 1962); Let Me Go The Right Way/Time Changes Things (Motown 1034, 1962); My Heart Can't Take No More/You Bring Back Memories (Motown 1040, 1963); A Breathtaking Guy/(The Man With The) Rock'n'Roll Banjo Band (Motown 1044, 1963); When The Lovelight Starts Shining Through His Eyes/Standing At The Crossroads Of Love (Motown 1051, 1963); Run, Run, Run/I'm Giving You Your Freedom (Motown 1054, 1964); Where Did Our Love Go/He Means The World To Me (Motown 1060, 1964); Baby Love/Ask Any Girl (Motown 1066, 1964); Come See About Me/(You're Gone But) Always In My Heart (Motown 1068, 1964); Stop In The Name Of Love/I'm In Love Again (Motown 1074, 1965); Back In My Arms Again/Whisper You Love Me Boy (Motown 1075, 1965); Nothing But Heartaches/He Holds His Own (Motown 1080, 1965); I Hear A Symphony/Who Could Ever Doubt My Love (Motown 1083, 1965); Twinkle Twinkle Little Me/Children's Christmas Song (Motown 1085, 1965); My World Is Empty Without You/Everything Is Good About You (Motown 1089, 1965); Love Is Like An Itching In My Heart/He's All I Got (Motown 1094, 1966); You Can't Hurry Love/Put Yourself In My Place (Motown 1097, 1966); You Keep Me Hangin' On/Remove This Doubt (Motown 1101, 1966); Love Is Here And Now You're Gone/There's No Stopping Us Now (Motown 1103, 1967); The Happening/All I Know About You (Motown 1107, 1967).

Diana Ross and the Supremes
Reflections/Going Down For The Third Time (Motown 1111, 1967); In And Out Of Love/I Guess I'll Always Love You (Motown 1116, 1967); Forever Came Today/Time Changes Things (Motown 1122, 1968); Some Things You Never Get Used To/You've Been So Wonderful To Me (Motown 1126, 1968); Love Child/Will This Be The Day (Motown 1135, 1968); I'm Living In Shame/I'm So Glad I Got Somebody (Like You Around) (Motown 1139, 1969); The Composer/The Beginning Of The End (Motown 1146, 1969); No Matter What Sign You Are/The Young Folks (Motown 1148, 1969); Someday We'll Be Together/He's My Sunny Boy (Motown 1156, 1969).

Diana Ross and the Supremes and the Temptations
I'm Gonna Make You Love Me/A Place In The Sun (Motown 1137, 1968); I'll Try Something New/The Way You Do The Things You Do (Motown 1142, 1969); The Weight/For Better Or Worse (Motown 1153, 1969).

Albums
Meet The Supremes (Motown 606, 1963); Where Did Our Love Go (Motown 621, 1964); A Little Bit Of Liverpool (Motown 623, 1964); The Supremes Sing Country, Western And Pop (Motown 625, 1965); We Remember Sam Cooke (Motown 629, 1965); More Hits (Motown 627, 1965); At The Copa (Live!) (Motown 636, 1965); Merry Christmas (Motown 638, 1965); I Hear A Symphony (Motown 643, 1966); Supremes A Go Go (Motown 649, 1966); The Supremes Sing Holland-Dozier-Holland (Motown 650, 1967); The Supremes Sing Rodgers And Hart (Motown 659, 1967); Greatest Hits Vols 1 and 2 (Motown 663, 1967).

Diana Ross and the Supremes
Reflections (Motown 665, 1968); Sing And Perform Funny Girl (Motown 672, 1968); Love Child (Motown 670, 1969); Live At London's Talk Of The Town (Motown 676, 1968); Let The Sunshine In (Motown 689, 1969); Cream Of The Crop (Motown 694, 1969); Greatest Hits Vol 3 (Motown 702, 1969); Farewell (Motown 708, 1970).

Diana Ross and the Supremes and the Temptations
Diana Ross And The Supremes Join The Temptations (Motown 679, 1968); TCB (Motown 682, 1968); Together (Motown 692, 1969); On Broadway (Motown 699, 1969).

Below: Mary Wilson (top) with Seventies Supremes Payne (left) and Green.

VALLI'S EVERGREENS

Why the Four Seasons were perennial chart-toppers

THE FOUR SEASONS STORY began in 1952 when the group's guiding hand and lead vocalist, Frankie Valli, started his singing career. He was born Francis Castellucio in Newark, New Jersey on 3 May 1937, and his early influences were blues, R&B and particularly the doo-wop tradition of the Eastern seaboard. His first engagements involved performing standards and novelties in neighbourhood bars and, within a year, he had caught the eye of Mercury Records' Paul Kapp. He released two singles on the label; one, 'My Mothers Eyes', appeared under the name of Frankie Valley, and the second, 'Somebody Else Took Her Home', as Frank Tyler and the Travellers, but neither met with any success and Valli took a day job.

In 1955 he auditioned for the lead vocalist position in a local group called the Variety Trio, whose line-up consisted of Nick and Tommy DeVito and Hank Majewski. Valli's arrival necessitated a change of name; first, the group became the Variatones and then, in 1956, they became the Four Lovers. A year of playing current hits, country and western and Italian favourites led to a recording contract with RCA.

Previously obliged to perform in a variety of styles to earn their daily bread, the Four Lovers were now able to record in their favoured doo-wop vocal style. They came along in the first wave of white doo-woppers like the Crewcuts, the Diamonds and the Three Chuckles and managed to pre-empt the competition by a few months when their first release, 'You're The Apple Of My Eye', charted nationally at Number 62 in 1956. The tune was written for them by noted songsmith Otis Blackwell.

Despite an album release and other singles, the summer of 1957 saw them back where they started; the Lovers had been dropped by RCA, while a solitary

42

Left: Seventies Seasons – Frankie Valli (foreground) with, from left, Gerry Polci, Don Ciccione, John Paiva and Lee Shapiro. Above: Dick Clark presents Valli with a gold disc for 'Sherry', while producer Bob Crewe stands far right. Above right: The Four Lovers, with Nick DeVito on bass and Hank Majewski (second left). Right: The first Seasons line-up poses for the camera.

single for Epic failed to chart. In 1958 Valli left the group to try again as a solo act but, after one release on Okeh, 'I Go Ape' (not the Neil Sedaka song), he re-joined the Four Lovers. 'I Go Ape' was important in one respect, however, as it was written by Bob Crewe, another singer in much the same state of frustration as Valli. Having watched other New York vocal groups overtake the Four Lovers in popularity, Valli and Crewe kept in touch, despite the failure of 'I Go Ape', and in 1961 began to work together in earnest.

The Four Lovers had released several records under various names, including Frankie Valle and the Romans, from 1959 to 1961 while continuing the rounds of New Jersey night-clubs. Nick DeVito and Majewski departed to be replaced by Nick Massi and former Royal Teen, Bob Gaudio. Gaudio had written 'Short Shorts', a hit in 1958, and brought a much-needed creative ability to the group.

Finding the name

Joining forces with Crewe, this new line-up began building a reputation as back-up singers and demo performers. With Crewe and Gaudio co-writing, the group appeared on over 25 singles under such diverse names as the Village Voices, the Topics, Hal Miller and the Rays, Alex Alda and Turner Di Sentri. This rejuvenation prompted yet another change of name and the Four Seasons, one of New York's most prestigious restaurants, was chosen as having the right connotations. Under this name they recorded one single, 'Spanish Lace', for George Goldner's End label before negotiating with the Vee-Jay label to release Bob Gaudio's 'Sherry'.

'Sherry' was a particularly extreme example of falsetto-led harmony singing and took America and most of the world by storm. The speed with which it climbed to Number 1 in the USA had been experi-

enced before only by Elvis Presley, while the fact that it was manufactured by Chicago's Vee-Jay Records, a black-owned label that had specialised in the best of Chicago's blues and R&B artists, contributed to a widespread misapprehension. The song was black in feel, content and delivery, and many radio programmers were convinced that the group was black. An appearance on Dick Clark's 'American Bandstand' television show (and a reputed following day's sales of 180,000 copies) both resolved the mystery and established the four clean-cut New Jersey Italians as the most popular vocal group in America literally overnight.

Falsetto singing had been immensely popular with urban black teenagers during the Fifties doo-wop craze, but until now Valli's high vocal range had not been utilised to the full. 'Sherry' changed all that, and the Four Seasons adopted the style of groups and singers like Maurice Williams and the Zodiacs, Pookie Hudson and the Spaniels, Frankie Lymon and Little Anthony and simply exposed it to millions of teenagers via radio. They were white boys interpreting a black sound and the success of 'Sherry' opened a new chapter in the Four Seasons story.

Soaring and screaming

'Big Girls Don't Cry' reached Number 1 towards the end of 1962 and 'Walk Like A Man' made the top in March 1963. In-between came the Top Thirty Christmas ditty 'Santa Claus Is Coming To Town'. The Number 1 songs broke with tradition

by sounding completely different from each other, something quite alien in the thinking of most people producing for the teenage market. What enabled the Four Seasons to achieve this feat was the unmistakable sound of Frankie Valli's voice which soared, and screamed, lulled or harmonised as required. Like the Beach Boys on the West Coast and the Beatles, it was instantly recognisable.

The massive sales of the first singles led to a round of non-stop touring and constant TV appearances, but the group found time to secure two Top Ten albums, form publishing companies and turn themselves into a profit-sharing partnership. After the success of 'Sherry', the Seasons booked themselves into New York's Stea-Phillips studios to record for a solid week. The first two albums included versions of many of the songs they had previously demoed for Crewe under various names, together with versions of many recent doo-wop hits by their contemporaries. Among these re-recorded gems were 'Yes Sir That's My Baby' (the Sensations), 'Peanuts' (the Thrillers), 'Teardrops' (Lee Andrews and the Hearts), 'Apple Of My Eye' (the Four Lovers, thereby covering their own first hit), 'Sincerely' (the Moonglows) and 'Since I Don't Have You' (the Skyliners) – almost a crash course in doo-wop for the uninitiated. It was their own songs, however, which were to make the group's reputation over the ensuing years and these came from the pens of Gaudio and Crewe.

Battle of the bands

'Sherry' hit the US charts around the same time that 'Love Me Do' by the Beatles peaked in the UK. Although the Seasons' first three singles all made the UK Top Twenty, the onslaught of Merseybeat during 1963 effortlessly removed the Italian-Americans from the British consciousness and they only toured the UK once, very briefly in early 1963. But it was through Bob Gaudio, who saw the potential of the Beatles and persuaded the executives of Vee-Jay to negotiate for American release, that the label obtained the rights to early Beatles material. Vee-Jay even released a 'battle of the bands' double album of Beatles and Seasons material in 1964, but by then both acts had left the label.

When Capitol Records finally broke the Beatles with 'I Want To Hold Your Hand' in early 1964, virtually every US act of note was washed away in the tidal wave of the British invasion; the Four Seasons and the Beach Boys stood almost alone. The Seasons' February 1964 release 'Dawn (Go Away)' stalled at Number 3 in the Hot Hundred with the Beatles at Numbers 1, 2, 4 and 5. But in July, 'Rag Doll' reached Number 1 and went on to sell a million copies.

'Dawn' was their first release on the Philips label; the group had left Vee-Jay in 1963 with a flurry of law suits over royalty payments. This was not what Valli and Gaudio had really wanted, however. The Seasons were at that time the biggest act in America, entirely self-contained in the fields of writing, production and arrangement. In what was very possibly the first negotiation of its kind in American record history, Atlantic Records offered them their own label and distribution. Such virtual autonomy was unheard-of in 1963, but DeVito and Massi were less sure of the public's loyalty and demanded too much money. The deal fell through.

Nick Massi left the group in 1965 to be replaced by Joe Long, and this new line-up entered 1966 with the Seasons at the peak of their career. In addition to their own hits, they had reached the Top Five with 'Don't Think Twice It's All Right', a version of the Bob Dylan song utilising Valli's impression of black jazz singer Rose Murphy. It had been released under the *nom de disque* of the Wonder Who, supposedly to prove the record would sell without the aid of the Seasons' name.

In another profitable diversification, Valli scored a major hit as a solo artist. After a few attempts with 'The Proud One', 'You're Gonna Hurt Yourself' and

Above: Frankie Valli unleashes his incomparable falsetto. Below: A mid-Sixties Seasons formation on stage. Despite changing line-ups, the group's vocal abilities remained unrivalled.

'You're Ready Now', Gaudio wrote him a song that has since become a *bona fide* standard in 'Can't Take My Eyes Off You'. It reached Number 2 and opened the door to Valli's career as a middle-of-the-road performer.

Although they had held off the English invasion, the Beatles and psychedelia, the Four Seasons were finally beaten by the Woodstock generation in 1969. *Genuine Imitation Life Gazette* was a project forced on the group by Gaudio and attempted to bring the group's vocal talents to bear on more serious material. It received a critical mauling. The album was enormously expensive to produce – its sleeve was a landmark in design – and it led indirectly to their split from producer Bob Crewe, Gaudio taking over his duties. Attempts to revive the Seasons' career with more pop-sounding material failed and the Philips contract ended in a repeat performance of their Vee-Jay departure.

As with Vee-Jay, however, they were able to buy back their masters and, despite the lack of immediate success and no recording contract, they toured as an oldies act. In 1970 DeVito left and, in what was a move of great business acumen, was bought out of all his royalty and publishing interests. Valli and Gaudio now owned the entire operation.

The Motown connection

After DeVito's departure, the group signed to Motown at the personal invitation of Berry Gordy with a contract negotiated between Valli and Gordy. The promise was that Gordy, a longtime fan, would personally guide their return to fame on the newly-founded Mowest label. As it happened, he was sidetracked by Diana Ross and her role as Billie Holiday in the film *Lady Sings The Blues*, and the whole period from 1971 to 1973 was almost a complete disaster from the Seasons' viewpoint. The one album, *Chameleon*, was a brilliant exercise in 1972 West Coast pop – a strange departure for a group who were for many years the 'sound of New York' – which received massive critical acclaim but miniscule sales.

At this time things were happening in the UK. The Northern soul circuit had picked up on Valli's solo 'You're Ready Now', and it reached the UK Number 11 position when reissued. The Four Seasons toured there for the first time since 1963 to great success, but their return to

America brought further problems. The Motown situation deteriorated, while a long-standing ear complaint threatened Valli with deafness. Joe Long left the fold, and Valli was now getting through seasons as quickly as the calendar; upwards of 10 musicians became Four Seasons between 1972 and 1976.

Valli countered Motown's refusal to release the group's greatest hits by licensing them to a TV merchandising company, Longines, which proceeded to sell 800,000 four-record sets. In 1974 Gaudio and Valli bought back the master of the only Motown recording they believed in, 'My Eyes Adored You', and this, along with the back catalogue, was licensed to Private Stock Records. In a year of concerted promotional effort, the label finally took the single to Number 1 in the US chart in 1975 and Valli signed as a solo artist, while the Four Seasons were reconstituted with new personnel.

The year 1975 was almost 1966 all over again, with Motown taking a track from

Chameleon, 'The Night', into the UK Top Ten, Valli's 'My Eyes Adored You' selling well and Warner's 'Who Loves You' by the new Four Seasons hitting on both sides of the Atlantic. Follow-ups and albums came in 1976, with 'December 1963' and 'Silver Star' being taken from the Warners *Who Loves You* album, and 'Swearin' To God', 'Fallen Angel' and 'Our Day Will Come' charting for Valli. He scored a US Number 1 with 'Grease' two years later, after the successful film of that title.

During this hectic period the Four Seasons' song catalogue had come in for heavy exploitation from the Bay City Rollers ('Bye Bye Baby'), Donny Osmond ('The Proud One', 'C'mon Marianne') and the Detroit Spinners ('Working My Way Back To You') among many others.

The follow-up LP to *Who Loves You* was released in April 1977. Entitled *Helicon*, it featured the same personnel as previously – Gerry Polci (drums), Don Ciccione (bass), Lee Shapiro (keyboards), John Paiva (guitar) and Valli – but failed to emulate its predecessor's commercial success. A cover of 'We Can Work It Out' for the Lou Reisner-produced album of Beatles songs, *All This And World War Too,* had provided a pleasant diversion late the previous year.

Frankie Valli's association with the Four Seasons ended for a short time in 1977 when he devoted himself once more to a solo career. As drummer Gerry Polci had shared some of the lead vocals, it seemed that the Seasons could survive well enough on their own. But this separation was short-lived, probably as much for publicity reasons as anything and Valli was back with the Seasons for a 1981 double album recorded live at Madison Square Garden. Bob Gaudio had retired from performing in 1974 to concentrate on production, though he continued to write for the Seasons.

By combining the joyous, uplifting feel of doo-wop with an evolving series of backing styles, the Seasons have enjoyed consistent success without compromise. From the clearly Spector-influenced castanets in 'Rag Doll' through the bass-driven dance-floor drive of 'The Night' to the bright disco rhythms of the *Who Loves You* LP, the music has never sounded dated. Yet it is the unmistakeable Valli falsetto, showcased in painstaking vocal arrangements, that has always been the instantly recognisable feature of each and every Four Seasons release. Their sound will live on as the sound of Sixties' teenage America.
BOB FISHER

The partnership of writer/producer Bob Gaudio (below) and lead singer Frankie Valli (below right) guided the Seasons into the Seventies. A chart renaissance in 1975 saw them return to the stage (below).

**Four Seasons
Recommended Listening**

The Four Seasons Story (Private Stock Records 1 C188-97 293/94) (A double-album compilation of Sixties hits including: Sherry, Big Girls Don't Cry, Walk Like A Man, Dawn, Ronnie, Rag Doll, Big Man In Town, Let's Hang On, Opus 17 (Don't You Worry 'Bout Me), I've Got You Under My Skin, C'mon Marianne); *Frankie Valli And The Four Seasons Revisited Live* (Warner Brothers Records K66098) (A four-sided album of live versions of old numbers as well as more recent hits which include December '63 (Oh What A Night) and Silver Star).

NATURAL HIGH

Lionel Richie took the Commodores to the top

It was during the first week of February 1969 that the Commodores, then merely a group of young musicians fresh out of college, made their first recordings. The studio was New York's Groove Sound, the producer was Jerry Williams Jr (also known as Swamp Dogg) and the record label was Atlantic.

Most of the session consisted of versions of contemporary hits such as Johnnie Taylor's 'Who's Making Love', Sly Stone's 'Sing A Simple Song', the Intruders' 'Cowboys To Girls' and Alvin Cash's 'Keep On Dancing'. Atlantic issued only the last-named tune, a funky but anonymous instrumental, and it disappeared without trace.

By 1971, however, the same group had secured a new recording deal – this time with Motown – and an opening spot on the Jackson Five's Madison Square Garden concert in July. These two career milestones eventually led the Commodores to become one of the hottest properties in black music.

Between 1974 and 1981, the Commodores reached the Top Ten of *Billboard*'s soul charts with 14 releases, including six that went to the top. More significantly, nine of these soul hits also made the pop Top Ten, broadening the band's popularity and boosting album sales.

The Commodores were almost as popular abroad, thanks to extensive touring. Early acceptance in Africa (Nigeria, in particular) and Asia (Japan, the Philippines) was gradually followed by popularity elsewhere, and by the late Seventies the group's visits to Europe were generating standing-room-only audiences.

Into the Mystics

To hear singer Lionel Richie tell the story, however, the Commodores were formed (in 1967 in Tuskegee, Alabama) as much to meet girls as to make music and money. Being in a band, he said, would guarantee them the favourable attention of Tuskegee

Ashburn managed to secure the Jackson Five support gig through a neighbourhood acquaintance, Suzanne DePasse, who worked for Motown. By this time, Callahan and Gilbert had departed to be replaced by drummer Walter Orange and bassist Ronald LaPread.

Performing with the Jacksons in New York and elsewhere immediately gave the Commodores valuable experience and exposure, but the recording deal did not pay off so promptly. Part of the problem lay with the various writers and producers – Tom Baird, Jeffrey Bowen, Gloria Jones and Pam Sawyer – Motown assigned to the group. The lack of a regular producer made it difficult for the group to create an identifiable sound.

Platinum hooks

The breakthrough eventually came in 1974 with 'Machine Gun', a rapid-fire, synthesiser-driven instrumental produced by James Carmichael that reached Number 22 in the US and Number 20 in Britain. The Commodores followed it with several similar exercises in high-energy funk, including 'The Zoo (The Human Zoo)', 'I Feel Sanctified' and 'Slippery When Wet'.

James Carmichael, like Benny Ashburn, proved to be a key figure in the Commodores' creative evolution. He was highly versatile, and a better arranger than other producers with whom they had worked; this became important when the success of 'Sweet Love', the act's first Top Ten pop hit in the States, suggested that their crossover chances were best with ballads. Carmichael crafted mellow, soulful arrangements to the lyrics and music of Lionel Richie, resulting in a series of major hits: 'Just To Be Close To You' (1976), 'Easy' (1977), 'Three Times A Lady' (a transatlantic chart-topper in 1978) and 'Sail On' (1979).

Although Richie's romantic songs turned out to be the most commercial, the Commodores continued to deliver up-tempo funk aimed predominantly at their black fans, and tunes such as 'Brick House' and 'Too Hot Ta Trot' were particularly popular in concert.

Each member contributed to the group's repertoire – and profited from it: in 1969, the six musicians, along with Ashburn, had formed the Commodores Entertainment Corporation (CEC) to handle their careers and income. In 1980, the company grossed more than 10 million dollars through interests in touring, recording, publishing, licensing, transportation, management and real estate.

The popularity of the Commodores generated substantial income for Motown, too, thereby ensuring its full and enthusiastic support of all the group's releases. In addition, two acts managed by CEC, Platinum Hook and Three Ounces of Love, recorded for the label.

The Commodores' fortunes began changing in 1980, however. Their tenth album, *Heroes*, failed to deliver a Top Ten hit single and, consequently, failed to match the sales of its predecessors. And although the group's next LP, *In The Pocket* (1981), returned them to hitmaking form, it was apparent that their most valuable commodity, Lionel Richie, was increasingly preoccupied by solo projects: first with country-pop crooner Kenny Rogers, for whom he wrote and produced 'Lady', and then with the music for Franco Zeffirelli's movie *Endless Love*.

In August 1981, Richie became the first artist in US chart history to appear in the Top Ten as composer, performer and/or producer of three simultaneous hits: Kenny Rogers' 'I Don't Need You' (which he produced), the Commodores' 'Lady (You Bring Me Up)' (which he co-produced and on which he sang lead vocal), and the title track from *Endless Love* (which he wrote, produced, and performed in duet with Diana Ross).

For their part, other members of the Commodores also engaged in various solo projects. Ronald LaPread, who had previously worked with another young band from Tuskegee called Seventh Wonder, produced A Taste of Honey. Milan Williams handled country singer Stella Parton, sister of Dolly, while Thomas McClary got involved with Klique (producing their first major hit, 'Stop Doggin' Me Around') and Michael Henderson.

It was the media attention paid to Lionel Richie's solo achievements, however, that created the most stress within the group. There was constant speculation that he would be leaving, and matters were not improved by the death of the Commodores' mentor, Benny Ashburn, in August 1982. Richie finally made his move several months later, and put his career in the hands of Kenny Rogers' manager. A highly successful solo album, *Lionel Richie* (1982), followed. 1983 saw the release of *Can't Slow Down*, while a single, 'All Night Long (All Night)', made Top Tens worldwide.

Now we are 13

The remaining Commodores, meanwhile, came up with a new album, *13* (1983). With Richie's sensuous ballads gone from the repertoire, the band went for a more energetic feel, with Walter Orange and Harold Hudson (a member of the group's brass section, Mean Machine) contributing vocals. 'Lionel deserved to be the focal point,' commented McClary, 'but the general feeling is we are now more entertaining – the group has a chance to diversify and show what we can offer collectively.' With this positive attitude, and stacks of talent, the Commodores seemed set for continuing success in the Eighties.
ADAM WHITE

The Commodores (above) were one of Motown's most successful acts of the Seventies. Unlike their Sixties predecessors, who were purely vocal groups backed by Motown house musicians, the Commodores played their own instruments. Singer and keyboardist Lionel Richie (inset above) later enjoyed a phenomenally successful solo career.

Institute's female campus members.

Richie, Thomas McClary (guitar) and William King (trumpet) originally played together as the Mystics before being joined by keyboard-player Milan Williams from another Tuskegee act, the Jays. With a couple of other musicians, Andre Callahan and Michael Gilbert, they became the Commodores and set their sights on professional opportunities in New York.

Those opportunities began to materialise when the group was spotted by Benny Ashburn, a public relations man and a former marketing executive with Pepsi-Cola. Having obtained a number of local night-club bookings for the Commodores,

The Commodores Recommended Listening

Zoom (Motown STMS 5061) (Includes: Squeeze The Fruit, Heaven Knows, Brick House, Won't You Come Dance With Me, Funny Feelings, Patch It Up); *Greatest Hits* (Motown STML 12100) (Includes: Three Times A Lady, Zoom, Slippery When Wet, Easy, Flying High, Just To Be Close To You).

Stratospheric soul from the Temptations

OF ALL THE GREAT soul groups of the Sixties, the Temptations were perhaps the most accomplished. Their influence is undeniable, their ability to survive the vagaries of fashion and vicissitudes of fortune no less remarkable. Most of their members came from the South. Paul Williams and Edward James Kendricks were both born in Birmingham, Alabama, in 1939, on 2 July and 7 December respectively. Together they founded the Primes, a group modelled on the Cadillacs, the Teenagers and other Fifties heroes. In Detroit, the group re-formed with the addition of Otis Williams (real name Otis Miles) and Melvin Franklin (David English).

Otis Williams entered the world in Texarkana, Texas, on 30 October 1941, and Franklin was born in Montgomery, Alabama, on 12 October 1942. Resettled in Detroit, they worked as Otis Williams and the Distants, together with Melvin's cousin Richard Street, a local boy born on 5 October 1942, and recorded for Northern Records. In 1960 Richard Street moved to Thelma Records as a producer. The Distants were now part of the Primes, and Street's place was taken by the enigmatic Elbridge Bryant. The group worked with LuPine as session singers and the same year were renamed the Temptations.

Their first singles, cut for Miracle Records, were 'Oh Mother Of Mine' (1961) and the testifying 'Check Yourself' (1962). The latter, written by the group with budding local record mogul Berry Gordy, was a modest hit and resulted in his signing them to Motown. The same year they made their debut on Motown's Gordy subsidiary label with the achingly beautiful 'Dream Come True'. The follow-up, 'Paradise', was anachronistic doo-wop written and produced by Gordy. Coupled with a typically neat Smokey Robinson song 'Slow Down Heart' it slid from view, and Elbridge Bryant left.

Rough'n'smooth

A formula was emerging. Trade a light tenor against someone with a gutbucket rasp, allow both moments of chilling falsetto, let them swap leads and anchor the result in impeccable harmonies from the rest of the group. This required vocal performers of equal stature, and it augured well when baritone David Ruffin moved from Miracle Records and slipped into Bryant's shoes. Ruffin, too, was from the South – Meridian, Mississippi, to be precise – where he was born on 8 January 1941.

Just how well he fitted was clear from 'I Want A Love I Can See', this time produced by its composer Smokey Robinson with proper respect for the church sound of the group. Issued in 1963, it sold sparsely but had a raw quality that indicated that the combination of producer Smokey Robinson with the Temptations would bear watching. After 'May I Have This Dance?', a Latin lilter produced by Gordy with writing contributions from the fledgling

Norman Whitfield, Robinson pitched in with 'The Way You Do The Things You Do', a loping stunner with tenor Kendricks riding high. During February 1964 it reached Number 11 in the Hot Hundred.

'I'll Be In Trouble', backed with 'The Girl's Alright With Me', consolidated their success. The top deck coasted under the guidance of Robinson, while an even more accomplished reverse introduced Norman Whitfield as producer. It lodged at Number 33 in May, and Whitfield continued at the helm for 'Girl (Why You Wanna Make Me Blue?)' which made Number 26 during September.

At the close of the year, the Temptations were appearing at the Apollo, New York, with Smokey Robinson and the Miracles. Both groups were worrying about new material; during an interval backstage Smokey sat down with Ronald White of the Miracles and teased out a new ballad, 'My Girl'. On reflection – and after some persuasion – he decided it might suit the Temptations. Risking Ruffin's raw voice on such a delicate song paid handsomely. Ethereal, tense and muscular by turns, 'My Girl' soared to Number 1 in both the pop and R&B charts during January 1965, giving the Temptations a million-seller and international acclaim.

'It's Growing', culled from *The Temptations Sing Smokey* collection, provided a sequel and reached Number 18 nationally during April 1965. Beautifully convoluted, it displayed a rare delicacy of structure. Robinson continued in his role as producer and composer with the dramatic string-kissed ballad 'Since I Lost My Baby', which registered at Number 17 in July 1965.

Later in the year, more Robinson material was taken from the *Temptin' Temptations* set for single release with the coupling of 'My Baby' and '(You Gotta Walk) Don't Look Back'. (The latter was revived in 1977 and given a reggae treatment by Peter Tosh.) The single enjoyed considerable success, peaking at Number 13 nationally.

Shimmer and strut

By now the Temptations were hot property. David Ruffin was the biggest sex symbol since Sam Cooke, and the group's beautifully-choreographed stage act had them gliding, turning, shimmering and walking with passionate precision. Every move was calculated as they turned immaculate cuffs and gleaming links to the lights. Robinson gave them the sweating 'Get Ready', tailor-made for the group to strut their stuff with Kendricks floating above. A US Number 29, it was a measure of its potency that it could still make Number 10 in the UK three years later.

'Ain't Too Proud To Beg' marked the coming of age of producer Norman Whitfield, who wrote it with Eddie Holland. It reached Number 13 in May 1966, and Whitfield seemed unstoppable. 'Beauty Is Only Skin Deep' was followed by '(I Know) I'm Losing You'; both were US Top Ten pop hits and made the Top Twenty on the other side of the Atlantic. The run continued with 'You're My Everything' and 'It's You That I Need', which haunted the upper echelons of the charts during 1967.

Then, in January 1968, came the million-selling 'I Wish It Would Rain', a single of enormous significance for the Temptations. Written by Whitfield with veteran Barrett Strong and performed with brooding power by Ruffin, its overture of crying seagulls and the storm breaking at the end demonstrated Whitfield's growing preoccupation with special effects. Purists have dated the decline of the group from this single, excellent though it was, and the fact that it made Number 4 in the American pop charts seemed to support the argument that they were moving too far from their soul roots.

While the album of the same name followed the single up the charts, David Ruffin decided to quit. His place was taken by Dennis Edwards from the Contours. Meanwhile, the rest of the group were becoming resentful at their lack of creative control. Accordingly, Otis Williams and Eddie Kendricks urged Whitfield to seek a more contemporary, adventurous format. They could not have foreseen the outcome. When Whitfield obliged with the million-selling 'Cloud Nine' – a US Number 6 and UK Number 15 – the Temptations unwittingly donned a new strait-jacket.

Psychedelic confusion

In the main it was the sound that mattered, the rich textures rather than the crass limitations of titles like 'Psychedelic Shack', a Number 7 US hit in 1970. Some, like the million-selling US Number 3 'Ball Of Confusion', were reasonably coherent message songs which successfully updated the Temptations' gospel roots. And despite the computerised slickness of albums like *Puzzle People*, *Psychedelic Shack* and *The Sky's The Limit*, there were still traditional soul gems like 'Just My Imagination', which topped the Hot Hundred during February 1971 to give Kendricks one of his best outings.

At this juncture Eddie Kendricks decided to pursue a solo career on the Tamla label, which he did with distinction for seven years, riding high in the national chart with 'Keep On Truckin'' (a 1973 Number 1) and 'Boogie Down' (Number 2 in 1974), before fading on Arista and Atlantic. When Rick Owens of the Vibrations failed to fill Kendricks' shoes, Damon Otis Harris was drafted in. Born in Baltimore on 17 July 1950 and raised on the gospel circuit, he had valuable R&B experience working with the Tempos and the Young Vandals. About the same time, Paul Williams finally succumbed to alcoholism; and Richard Street, who had been singing with the Monitors, returned to the fold after a decade's absence.

Whitfield's increasingly grandiose conceptions, including *Solid Rock* (1971), *All Directions* (1972) and the blindingly-conceited *Masterpiece* (1973) all but eclipsed the group as a vocal unit. Never-

Eddie Kendricks (above) left the Temptations in the Seventies to pursue a solo career, which brought him a US Number 1 hit, 'Keep On Truckin''.

theless he should not be denied his moment. 'Papa Was A Rolling Stone', from *All Directions*, and 'Ma', from *Masterpiece*, were strokes of genius, where Whitfield succeeded in marrying blues roots, narrative and neo-soul in a shimmering contemporary sound. 'Papa' topped the US national charts, made Number 14 in Britain and thoroughly merited its Grammy for best R&B single of 1972. And 'Hurry Tomorrow' from *Masterpiece* gave Damon Harris a substantial showcase when it was released as a single. An unequivocal anti-drug tirade of great power and subtlety, it set the record straight for all those who had worried about Whitfield's flirtation with the junkie subculture.

In 1974 the *1990* album found the Temptations still locked in Whitfield's fantasy, and the producer's undoubted energy was increasingly given over to projects with the Undisputed Truth, Rare Earth and Yvonne Fair. The group then turned to producer Jeffrey Bowen, but the album which followed, *A Song For You*, was unexceptional. In the middle of the following year Damon Harris left for Philadelphia. His replacement in the Temptations was Glenn Leonard.

At the close of 1976 the group moved to Atlantic. Dennis Edwards dropped out, making room for the nephew of R. H. Harris of the Soul Stirrers. Louis Price was born in 1953, raised in Chicago and, like his famous uncle, worked the gospel trail. He came to the Temptations after a spell with Jerry Butler's workshop and, like Leonard, he was to be a useful member of the group. The Atlantic label was not so useful, however. Despite recording in

Philadelphia, New York and LA, the end product was disappointing. Merely competent was not good enough for an erstwhile supergroup, and after two albums, *Hear To Tempt You* (1977) and *Bare Back* (1978), the Temptations returned to Motown. At the same time Dennis Edwards reclaimed his place.

Their homecoming album, *Power*, produced in Los Angeles by Angelo Bond, made ripples in 1980 but it was left to Thom Bell in the autumn of 1981 to make waves with an album simply called *The Temptations*. Cut in Philadelphia and Seattle, it was a minor classic, especially cleansing after Whitfield's excesses, and yielded an interesting single in the silky chamber soul of 'The Life Of A Cowboy'.

The way was paved for the massive success of *Reunion* in May 1982. The title was not misleading: to the line-up of Otis Williams, Dennis Edwards, Glenn Leonard, Richard Street and Melvin Franklin were restored the proven talents of Eddie Kendricks and David Ruffin, while top producers, including Rick James, Smokey Robinson and Barrett Strong, were employed. On ballads like Ron Miller's 'I've Never Been To Me' they equalled the definitive Nancy Wilson reading of 1977. And one track, Rick James' 'Standing On The Top', gave them a funk single of devastating force. For longevity and range the Temptations have no equals; throughout their career they both led and absorbed the changes in soul.

CLIVE ANDERSON

**The Temptations
Recommended Listening**

20 Golden Greats (Tamla Motown STML 12140) (Includes: Just My Imagination, I Second That Emotion, Ain't Too Proud To Beg, Ball Of Confusion, Psychedelic Shack, Take A Look Around); *Masterpiece* (Tamla Motown STMS 5021) (Includes: Law Of The Land, Ma, Plastic Man, Hurry Tomorrow, Masterpiece).

YOUNG, GIFTED AND BLACK
YOUNG, GIFTED AND BLACK
YOUNG, GIFTED AND
YOUNG, GIFTED A
YOUNG, GIFTED

The rise and rise of the Jackson Five

THE LIST OF TALENT that Berry Gordy, founder and owner of Motown Record Corporation, has been able to secure over the years has been quite extensive and impressive. Marvin Gaye, Stevie Wonder, Diana Ross, the Supremes and the Commodores immediately spring to mind as acts that have reached international status. To these must be added the Jackson Five, a group of brothers whose vibrant young black sound was nurtured by the Motown machinery to produce million-selling records.

The Jackson Five initially comprised five young brothers from Gary, Indiana; they were Michael (born 29 August 1959), Jermaine (born 11 December 1954), Sigmund Esco – known as 'Jackie' (born 4 May 1951), Marlon (born 12 March 1958) and Toriano Adaryll – known as 'Tito' (born 15 October 1953). Their younger brother, Randy (born 29 October 1962) joined them later, and they also had three sisters – Maureen, Latoya and Janet.

Their motivation came initially from their father, Joe Jackson, a crane operator who played in a local R&B band named the Falcons. He turned his own musical ambitions towards his children and encouraged them to learn to play instruments, putting them through daily rehearsals and grooming them for talent contests. Their mother, Katherine, was a blues and country singer. The brothers soon became a tight, polished and assured line-up with smooth dance routines, doing cover versions of Temptations, Sly Stone and Smokey Robinson numbers.

Lucky break

The group's first date was at a local club, Mr Lucky's, where they made five dollars from the audience pitching coins onto the floor. Joe Jackson booked his sons as a regular attraction on the club circuit where, during the school holidays, they supported such bands as Gladys Knight and the Pips and their heroes, the Temptations. He also secured a six-month recording contract with a local label, Steel Town, on which the brothers released one single in 1968 – 'I'm A Big Boy Now', produced by Gordon Keith. Two other early songs – 'Some Girls Want Me For Their Love' and 'You Don't Have To Be Over 21 To Fall In Love' – appeared on Dynamo in 1971 to capitalise on the brothers' success.

The Motown version of the Jacksons' success story plays on their 'discovery' by Diana Ross, promoting them through her by calling their first LP *Diana Ross Presents The Jackson Five* (1970). Admittedly, it was Ross who tipped Berry Gordy off about the family band when she was persuaded to see their show during her visit to Gary in 1968. At that time, Motown desperately needed another group to succeed commercially, as their Sixties acts the Temptations, the Four Tops and the Miracles ran out of steam.

The famous Five (above) were renowned for their colourful stage shows. From left: Tito, Marlon, Jackie, Michael and Jermaine. Previous page: The Jacksons, with Randy (left) replacing Jermaine.

The Jackson Five injected a fresh appeal to the Motown sound and brought them a new market of teenies and pre-teenies who could identify with the 10-year-old Michael. They were nice, clean-living, polite, good-looking boys who displayed energy and style and proved to be more than a mere bubblegum group. Their well-packaged image was backed up with a fair degree of musical talent – not just collectively, but in their solo careers, too.

The band's output included both poppy soul numbers and melodic, emotive ballads. The success of their fresh approach can be demonstrated by the hits they had with Bill Withers' 'Ain't No Sunshine' (by Michael Jackson) and Jackson Browne's 'Doctor My Eyes', the UK chart success of which eclipsed the original in both cases.

Motown signed up the Jackson Five early in 1969 and released their debut single, 'I Want You Back' (written by a collection of the company's top composers and producers known as the Corporation), in October. It was an international big-seller, making Number 2 in the UK charts, Number 1 in the States, and was arguably the best single the Jackson Five made. It had a tight Sly-influenced soul arrangement of bass, drums, piano and guitar, behind the unbroken voice of Michael, stretched to its bubbly heights. Follow-up singles achieved similar success – 'ABC', 'Mama's Pearl', 'The Love You Save', 'I'll Be There', 'Never Can Say Goodbye' and 'Doctor My Eyes'.

On stage the brothers wooed audiences with youthful energy, pulsating music and tightly-rehearsed dance routines, led by little Michael writhing around like a miniature James Brown. The Five were often augmented on stage by two cousins – Johnny Jackson on drums and Ronnie Rancifer on piano. They were to prove a model for the Osmonds, a young Mormon family unit who were later marketed as the Jackson Five's white counterparts.

Rockin' Michael

With fame came fortune, so the Jackson family moved to a 12-roomed mansion in the San Fernando Valley, California. The school-age brothers attended a nearby private school, with tutors accompanying them on tour. The group received unprecedented worldwide acclaim; the press reported their every move and word, a cartoon series devised around them was screened in America and England, and they hosted several American television specials.

Not content with the group's almost fairytale success, Motown decided to record certain brothers individually. Michael Jackson, being lead singer, was the first with the sweeping ballad 'Got To Be There' in October 1971, followed closely by an album of the same name. The album provided several million-selling singles such as 'Rockin' Robin' (a revival of Bobby Day's 1958 hit) and 'I Wanna Be Where You Are'. His solo chart run with Motown lasted, on and off, until 1981. Hot on Michael's heels was older brother, Jermaine, with 'That's The Way Love Goes' in August 1972, taken from his *Jermaine* album released four months later. Michael had little difficulty in securing chart hits;

Jermaine, on the other hand, found it hard going outside America.

Touring took up much of the group's time and energy, but it was a necessary part of their life which they both loved and hated. They attracted mass hysteria and fan worship in every country they visited. Meanwhile, the conveyor-belt hit formula continued with the singles 'Sugar Daddy' in November 1971 and 'Little Bitty Pretty One' (a cover of Bobby Day's 1957 hit) in April 1972. A change of musical style – an almost mature sound – arrived with 'Lookin' Through The Windows' in June 1972. That same month Michael Jackson's biggest-selling solo single, the title song from the movie *Ben*, was issued, with Jermaine's million-selling 'Daddy's Home' following in November. The group's next single, 'Corner Of The Sky', was more adventurous in style, with the chirpy 'Hallelujah Day' following early in 1973. Jackie was the third brother to embark on a solo career within the group with his first album, titled after himself, being issued in January 1974.

Farewell to Motown
It had become evident that the group's bubblegum soul sound was very much a part of their past. No longer was Motown assured of chart-topping albums and singles, and discontent grew within the group as the company's interest waned. This, combined with the ongoing argument caused by Berry Gordy's refusal to let the brothers expand as writers and producers, saw the Jackson Five join the exodus from Motown in 1975. Other big names on the move had included Mary Wells, Martha Reeves and Gladys Knight, and these departures inevitably led to legal battles over rights and contracts.

Motown retained the name Jackson Five and one of the brothers, Jermaine, whose marriage to Gordy's daughter, Hazel, in 1973 had been a much-publicised event, costing 200,000 dollars and featuring 175 doves and Smokey Robinson performing a specially-written song. Jermaine continued in his solo career and acted as Motown's talent scout; the other brothers signed a multi-million dollar deal with CBS/Epic as the Jacksons. The group formed two publishing companies – Peacock Music and Stone Gold Music – and obtained total control of all their recordings, while Randy took Jermaine's place in the ranks.

The brothers' stay at Motown had produced six platinum singles and 10 gold albums, with estimated worldwide sales of 100 million units. After their departure from the label, Motown continued to release their material in various re-packages backed up by special campaigns, their biggest coup being the UK chart-topping

Slick mover Michael was the master of the dance routine (overleaf), slipping into leather (left) for his 1983 video to sing that 'Billie Jean' was not his girl. Rumour hinted that Diana Ross (above left) was.

success in 1981 of Michael Jackson's 'One Day In Your Life', which had originally been issued in 1975.

The first Epic album, *The Jacksons*, was produced by Philadelphia's Kenny Gamble and Leon Huff and reached gold status. The brothers had wanted to work with the duo while at Motown, but Gordy had insisted on keeping recordings in-house. During 1977 the single 'Show Me The Way To Go' reached Number 1 in the UK. Motown were quick to cash in by issuing a three-track single containing 'Skywriter', 'I Want You Back' and 'The Love You Save'. *Goin' Places* was the second Epic album, again written and produced by Gamble and Huff, and the title track was lifted for single release at the close of 1977. Compared to the first release, this was uninspiring; it seemed the Jacksons/Philadelphia marriage was heading for the rocks. The group's initial CBS success was nowhere near that achieved in the heady days at Motown.

By 1979 Michael Jackson's interest had turned towards the film industry and he decided to take up an offer to appear in *The Wiz*, sharing top billing with Diana Ross. The film provided the uneventful single 'You Can't Win', produced by Quincy Jones (who was responsible for writing the musical score) in 1979. Later that year, with no new group material due, Michael went back into the studios with Jones to record his debut solo Epic album, *Off The Wall*. The LP, which featured session players the Brothers Johnson and songwriter Rod Temperton (of Heatwave), covered a wide spectrum of music and excelled on dance numbers as well as ballads like 'She's Out Of My Life'. 'Don't Stop Till You Get Enough' was the first of four singles taken from the album, all of which were Top Ten entrants on both sides of the Atlantic.

The album itself reached double platinum status and sold over four million copies. This astounding worldwide selling power affected Michael badly – he became rather reclusive and eccentric, unable to handle his daily life. As a solo artist he had reached massive heights, far beyond that previously enjoyed with the group. One offshoot of this success was that many artists sought to secure his writing and producing talents. Again Motown cashed in by releasing the Jackson Five's *20 Golden Greats* album which spanned material from 1969 to 1974.

The Jacksons' next LP was *Destiny* (1978), the title track being issued to coincide with a UK tour that formed part of a worldwide trek. The album was the first to be written and produced by the brothers, and this policy was to continue with future releases. By 1980 Michael had produced sister Latoya for Polydor, worked with a handful of other artists, and in 1981 won the R&B Grammy Award for the Best Male Vocal Performance, on 'Don't Stop Till You Get Enough'. That success wasn't allowed to pass by – Motown issued *The Best Of Michael Jackson* in its mid-priced album series. That wasn't the only time the two crossed, as the Jackson family paid Motown 100,000 dollars in settlement of the company's lawsuit against the group and CBS. The settlement, among other things, provided full usage by Motown of all Jackson Five and Michael Jackson product recorded during their Motown days.

Rumours of romance
October 1980 saw the release of *Triumph*, an album critics claimed was just that. This dance-oriented set was light on ballads, with 'Time Waits For No-One' being the most commercial. 'Lovely One' was the first single to be lifted, but 'Can You Feel It' was to prove the biggest-selling track. Michael hit the headlines at this time for his association with Diana Ross. He appeared on her 'Diana' television special and the romance on screen was said to be flourishing off-stage as well. Whatever the relationship, it did lead to him writing and producing Ross's 1982 hit single 'Muscles'.

The Jacksons as a group continued to go from strength to strength, and with the success came elusiveness. Interviews with the press, on radio or television became practically non-existent, and their closeness with their audiences was lost as they chose videos, rather than live performance, to promote their songs. Jermaine, meanwhile, had achieved a UK Top Ten hit single with Stevie Wonder's 'Let's Get Serious' in 1980.

In September 1982 Michael Jackson and ex-Beatle Paul McCartney collaborated to release 'The Girl Is Mine', a mediocre track that appeared on Jackson's second solo album, *Thriller* (1982). Jackson worked on the album with Quincy Jones, while Marlon produced tracks for Betty Wright. Meanwhile, the Jacksons released *The Jacksons Live* (1981), a double set recorded during an American tour.

Thriller provided Michael Jackson with the hit single 'Billie Jean' which was accompanied by a slick and imaginative video produced by Steve Barron, showing a rather more sophisticated and self-conscious Michael injecting an almost sobbing emotion into his vocals. The album may not have matched the brilliance of *Off The Wall*, but it nevertheless wasted no time soaring to the top of the album charts in both the UK and the States. 'Billie Jean' hurtled to Number 1 in the singles charts on both sides of the Atlantic, and 'Beat It', another track from the album, followed it into the US and UK Top Ten. With other big-name artists falling over themselves to work with him, Michael Jackson has certainly achieved his childhood ambition 'to become a big star'.   SHARON DAVIS

Michael Jackson and the Jackson Five Recommended Listening

Anthology (Motown TMSP 6004) (Includes: I Want You Back, ABC, Lookin' Through The Windows, Ben, Ain't No Sunshine, Rockin' Robin, Dancing Machine); *Off The Wall* (Epic EPC 83468) (Includes: Rock With You, Don't Stop Till You Get Enough, Girlfriend, Off The Wall, Burn This Disco Out, She's Out Of My Life).

The Solo Superstars

With increasing acclaim, came demands from Gordy's protégés for greater control over their material. From Gordy's standpoint the results of this freedom must have been viewed with ambivalence. On one hand, there was the huge artistic and commercial success of Marvin Gaye and Stevie Wonder and the consistent excellence of Smokey Robinson; on the other, the subsequent departures of Gaye and Diana Ross,

Exciting to watch on stage and creators of
records that throbbed with emotion,
Smokey Robinson and the Miracles
produced a sound that appealed to blacks
and whites alike.

The Miraculous Smokey Robinson

Was Smokey the real king of Motown?

IN THE LANDSCAPE of black music since the late Fifties the work of William 'Smokey' Robinson stands out for such milestones as 'Shop Around', 'You Really Got A Hold On Me', 'My Guy', 'My Girl', 'The Tracks Of My Tears' and 'Tears Of A Clown'. Robinson is a man of many accomplishments as songwriter, performer and producer. His formation of the Miracles, his role in the birth and development of Motown Records, and his later career as a solo artist mark him out as an exceptional talent and a potent influence on the course of popular music.

Born on 19 February 1940, William Robinson grew up in Detroit's poor North End, his father a truck-driver, his mother a government worker. Nicknamed Smokey by an uncle, he attended Dwyer Elementary, Hutchins Intermediate and Northern High schools, and wrote his first 'song' at the age of six for a school play.

Spurred by his mother's love of gospel and blues, Robinson became increasingly interested in music. 'I used to buy a lot of song-books with people like Snooky Lansen and Dean Martin on the covers,' he recalled, 'because I wanted to know the words of the current tunes that were popular. I would buy those rather than candy.'

His interest also extended to R&B performers such as Billy Ward's Dominoes and Nolan Strong and the Diablos. Soon the young Robinson and schoolfriends Ronnie White, Pete Moore and Bobby and Sonny Rogers formed their own group, the Matadors. 'We started singing in Junior High, and performed around Detroit at house parties, record hops, talent shows and school functions. Of course, there were groups all over the place; everyone was in one.' Robinson cited the Dominoes' Clyde McPhatter as a major influence; his high-pitched vocals reassured the teenager that his own falsetto singing style was worthy of pride.

Graduating from Northern High in June 1957, Smokey prepared to attend college the following January in pursuit of qualifications in electrical engineering. That August, however, he and his fellow Matadors heard of a local audition being staged by Jackie Wilson's manager to hear new talent with recording potential. Group member Sonny Rogers' decision to join the Army complicated matters, but a replacement was soon found in his sister, Claudette, who had been in the Matadors' distaff rivals, the Matadorettes.

The group's performance of 'four or five' numbers that August day failed to impress Wilson's manager, but did attract songwriter Berry Gordy, also present, who asked about one in particular, 'Mama Done Told Me'. Learning of Robinson's authorship of that and dozens of other compositions, the future founder of Motown offered the teenagers advice and work as backup vocalists on some of his independent productions.

Miraculous harmonies

Several months on, with the group renamed the Miracles, Gordy cut their first record, 'Got A Job', an answer to the Silhouettes' chart-topping doo-wop, 'Get A Job', and sold the master to End Records in New York. It was released in February 1958, attracting good notices in the trade press that apparently generated sales. A second End single, '(I Need Some) Money', went unnoticed.

The following year, Gordy and Robinson wrote and produced a new song, 'Bad Girl', and leased the result to Chicago's Chess Records for national distribution. It was an important disc for the Miracles. While Smokey's distinctive falsetto was a feature of 'Got A Job' and '(I Need Some) Money', both were uptempo items encumbered by distracting doo-wop harmonies. By contrast, 'Bad Girl' was a plaintive ballad, the perfect showcase for Robinson's aching, tremulous style, which was cleverly accentuated by a haunting flute motif.

The record performed well in several markets, even reaching *Billboard*'s Hot Hundred for a couple of weeks; according to Smokey, 'it was the one that started us on the road, doing professional dates.' Robinson made his debut at New York's Apollo Theatre on a bill headed by Ray Charles. 'We were so horrible that the promoter called Berry and said he didn't want to pay us. We didn't have any money, so we had to send for some just to get out of the hotel and back home.' Another disc, 'Don't Say Bye Bye' by Ron and Bill (Ronald White and Smokey Robinson), appeared on the Chess brothers' label, Argo, in 1959.

All the Miracles' recordings to this point were produced by Gordy himself, but when Robinson came off the road one day with a 'really hot tune', he and the group went into the studio on their own. The session proceeded well, and the song, 'Way Over

Inset far left: Checking out Smokey (second from right) and the Miracles. Inset left: Several years and many hits later, the smiles remain. Inset above: Berry Gordy (right) sees the Miracles off on tour. Below: The group on stage.

There', became the first Miracles disc nationally released on the Tamla label, rather than leased elsewhere. Although failing to make the charts it sold some 60,000 copies in a few months, sufficient to establish the new company's identity with key distributors. This became important when the group's next record was issued.

When Smokey Robinson originally wrote 'Shop Around', it was intended for Barrett Strong, the 'Money' hitmaker. Berry Gordy heard the song, made some structural changes and then persuaded Robinson to cut it himself with the Miracles. The record was scarcely in the hands of distributors when Gordy interrupted Robinson's sleep one night with a frantic phone call telling him to get down to the recording studios with the Miracles.

Robinson assembled the Miracles for that early hours recording session, and the new, improved version of 'Shop Around' was duly distributed to replace the first shipment. Gordy's instincts were proved correct the disc became a national hit, topping the R&B charts early in 1961 and climbing to Number 2 in the pop listings although the re-recording was not dramatically different from the original.

Smokey's energetic vocals and the harmonies provided by Claudette (whom he had just married), Ronnie, Pete and Bobby were almost identical, as was Ron Wakefield's midpoint saxophone solo. But the tune's tempo was faster, and Benny Benjamin's drums were more pronounced in the mix, even though he changed from sticks to brushes for the revision. The overall result served to emphasise Gordy's attention to detail and drive for perfection, which was to characterise so much of Motown's development in the years ahead.

Apart from helping to establish the company as a serious contender in the music marketplace, the success of 'Shop Around' put the Miracles' career on a firm footing. Subsequent releases in 1961 and 1962 achieved Top Twenty status in the R&B field; they included 'Ain't It Baby', 'Everybody's Gotta Pay Some Dues', 'What's So Good About Goodbye' and 'I'll Try Something New'. In each new recording, Smokey's aching falsetto seemed more soulful; in each new song, the imagery of his lyrics became more adventurous, more sophisticated.

Crossover success

Significant sales among white pop-buyers were harder to achieve than among black consumers, yet the group collected a couple of major crossover hits in 1963 with 'You've Really Got A Hold On Me', an impassioned, brooding ballad on which Smokey and Bobby Rogers shared lead vocals, and 'Mickey's Monkey', an exuberant, uptempo dance item penned for the Miracles by the then-fledgling team of Eddie Holland, Lamont Dozier and Brian Holland. Both records went Top Ten across the US, and 'You've Really Got A Hold On Me' travelled abroad to catch the attention of a young British rock band weaned on black music. The Beatles covered the song for their second album, and John Lennon named the Miracles as his favourite group.

The Miracles' American popularity was further enhanced by participation in the Motortown Revue, Berry Gordy's touring package as many as 10 acts per show, with Smokey and the group usually the headliners which criss-crossed the country week after week, month after month in the early Sixties. The revue constantly broke concert attendance records, and also fuelled the label's pursuit of the album market with a series of 'Recorded Live On Stage' LPs. It was during this period that Claudette Robinson retired from touring (although she continued to record with the group) and that Pete Moore took temporary leave of absence to serve in the US Army.

Throughout 1964 and early 1965, the Miracles sustained their reputation for strong, R&B-oriented material, balancing party-time items with straightforward love songs. More than before, Smokey began to write in collaboration with Peter Moore, Bobby Rogers and Ronnie White, and the 'sixth' Miracle, guitarist Marv Tarplin, became more active as a composer, too.

The results may be judged to represent Robinson's most creative period. His strength has always been in lyrics – Berry Gordy's early advice was 'let the songs mean something by themselves', without orchestration, without production – and it's arguable that increased collaboration with others provided a better melodic foundation for that strength. Tarplin's contribution, especially, was critical to the remarkable intensity and depth of Smokey and the Miracles' recordings between 1965 and 1967, which included 'Ooo Baby Baby', 'The Tracks Of My Tears', 'My Girl Has Gone', 'Choosey Beggar', 'Going To A Go-Go', 'A Fork In The Road' and 'The Love I Saw In You Was Just A Mirage'.

Robinson had become no less concerned with basic emotions of love and desire, happiness and heartbreak than in his early songs, but he employed increasingly subtle ways of expressing himself. And sadness seemed so often to prevail. 'I think more people identify with those type of songs,' he remarked. 'I guess my mind is just oriented towards that type of thought. You can start singing a happy song and it strikes a groove, it gets people happy. But the sad songs, they get the reaction.'

Nothing illustrates the point better than 'The Tracks Of My Tears', perhaps the quintessential Smokey lyric:

People say I'm the life of the party
  'cause I tell a joke or two
But though I might be laughing loud
  and hearty, deep inside I'm blue
So take a good look at my face
You'll see my smile is out of place
Just look closer and it's easy to trace
The tracks of my tears.

This period also produced the Miracles' most consistent run of major hit records. 'Ooo Baby Baby' was the first of a half-dozen singles to reach the Top Twenty of the US pop charts between May 1965 and April 1967 (those six also reached Top Ten status in the R&B market). In 1966, the group's *Going To A Go-Go* album went Top Ten pop and Number 1 R&B, and became the best-selling LP of the Miracles' career.

Founding Motown

As noted earlier, Smokey Robinson's role in the formation of Motown Records was more than just as leader of the company's first group. Only too eager to receive Berry Gordy's songwriting advice when they first met, he soon developed into a solid collaborator, working with his new friend and business colleague on material for such artists as Marv Johnson, Barrett Strong, Sammy Ward and the Contours, among other early Motown acts.

Robinson's moral support was vital, too. He recalls driving with Gordy through appalling winter weather in January 1959 to collect a few hundred first-run pressings of Marv Johnson's 'Come To Me' from a factory near Flint, Michigan. The journey nearly terminated Motown there and then: the car twice skidded off the ice-covered highway and into a ditch, once to avoid a head-on collision with a heavy truck.

But, most importantly, Robinson kept encouraging Gordy to go national with the company rather than continue 'test-marketing' product in Detroit which had to be leased to major labels for sales beyond the city. He kept reiterating their disappointing experience with other labels – the pitiful royalties paid by End Records, the failure by Chess to even release the 'Bad Girl' follow-up until 'Way Over There' started to sell.

Expanding responsibilities

Once Motown had established itself nationally with the Miracles and several subsequent acts, the company's roster began to expand. Robinson assumed responsibilities in artist development and production, working primarily with Mary Wells. 'I would say that she was the real starter for me, because I got the chance to do exactly as I pleased, you know, the songs any way I wanted them. It really put me in a new frame of mind as far as the business went.'

That frame of mind tapped the motherlode. Smokey penned and produced a stunning series of (mostly) midtempo ballads for Wells, which became major hits in both the pop and R&B categories: 'The One Who Really Loves You', 'You Beat Me To The Punch', 'Two Lovers', 'Laughing Boy', 'Your Old Stand-By' and 'My Guy'. The singer's light but expressive voice was the perfect vehicle for Robinson's romantic lyrics, and she was willing, even anxious, to be shown exactly what phrasing, what nuances to employ.

Another act newly signed to the company was less successful in Robinson's hands, despite the fact that it was he who auditioned Diana Ross, Mary Wilson,

Right: The post-Smokey Miracles, with new recruit Bill Griffin. Below: The same line-up in live action. Opposite above: Smokey's 1982 album, Yes It's You Lady.

Florence Ballard and Barbara Martin, and brought them to Berry Gordy's attention. Gordy himself produced the Supremes' first two Tamla singles, but Robinson handled three of their next four: 'Your Heart Belongs To Me', 'You Bring Back Memories' and 'A Breathtaking Guy'. All rather similar to his work with Mary Wells, 'A Breathtaking Guy' is the best, a melancholy melody anchored to a rolling rhythm track that's almost a Cha-Cha, sweetened by some unobtrusive brass. It only scraped the charts in August 1963, and the Supremes profitably switched producers to Holland/Dozier/Holland.

By this time a vice-president of Motown, Robinson was working with the Marvelettes. During 1963 and 1964 they had three modest sellers – 'As Long As I Know He's Mine', 'He's A Good Guy' and 'You're My Remedy' – but Robinson's next major success came with the Temptations.

Producing the Temptations

The group's first five releases (only one written by Smokey) had sold relatively few copies, but when Robinson and Bobby Rogers composed 'The Way You Do The Things You Do' while travelling home from New York one night, they were confident of breaking the Temptations into the big time. The song's endearing sequence of similes, Eddie Kendricks' arresting falsetto and Smokey's pounding production proved irresistible. The record went Top Twenty in April 1964.

It was merely the first. Robinson, collaborating periodically with Rogers, Pete Moore and Ronnie White, crafted a remarkable run of hits for the Temptations, each seemingly finer than the one before, each taking the group to new heights of commercial acceptance. Among memorable titles were 'I'll Be In Trouble', 'My Girl', 'It's Growing', 'Since I Lost My Baby', 'My Baby' and 'Get Ready'.

On most of these, David Ruffin's soulful declamation of Robinson's lyrics was central. The Miracles' leader had seen him perform at Detroit's Twenty Grand club shortly after he was recruited by the Temptations; Ruffin sang a Drifters tune, and Smokey was sufficiently impressed to write 'My Girl' as a showcase for his lead vocals. The disc became the group's first Number 1 hit.

Robinson's results with the Temptations only seemed to make him more prolific. Throughout 1965 and 1966 he wrote and produced hits for Marvin Gaye ('I'll Be Doggone', 'Ain't That Peculiar', 'One More Heartache', 'Take This Heart Of Mine'), the Marvelettes ('Don't Mess With Bill', 'You're The One', 'The Hunter Gets Captured By The Game'), Brenda Holloway ('When I'm Gone', 'Operator') and the Contours ('First I Look At The Purse'). There were also underrated items with Jimmy Ruffin ('As Long As There Is L-o-v-e') and Barbara McNair ('Here I Am Baby'), and a fine Supremes outing, 'Take Me Where You Go'.

As a producer, Robinson believed in giving the artists as much latitude as possible to interpret the song as they wished, to inject their own personality into the session. He says Marvin Gaye, in particular, seized that opportunity, which may account for the high voltage which runs through recordings like 'Ain't That Peculiar' and 'One More Heartache'.

Given the extent of Smokey's commitments during the Sixties, all undertaken while continuing his career with the Miracles, was his departure from the group inevitable? Robinson was adamant at the time, and remains so today, that life on the road dictated the decision – or, more accurately, life away from his family. Claudette suffered several miscarriages through the rigours of touring with the group in the early years, so when the couple's first child, Berry, was born in 1968, and daughter Tamla came two years later, it was only natural that Smokey should want to spend more time at home.

'I enjoyed the fact that I was with the Miracles. I had known them since I was very young, and so we had a brotherly love, a brotherly relationship. And I enjoyed being on stage performing. But I was becoming bored with life on the road: the packing and unpacking, the hotels and the restaurants, the airports and the bus stations. And I didn't want to be away from my children all the time, I didn't want them to know me only as a celebrity.'

Smokey Robinson and the Miracles (the billing was officially changed to that in 1967) didn't lack for hits in the last five years of their career together. Smokey was working with a new collaborator by this point, Al Cleveland, and the partnership yielded a major 1967 hit, 'I Second That Emotion', and only slightly smaller ones with 'Yester Love', 'Special Occasion', 'Baby Baby Don't Cry', 'Doggone Right' and 'Point It Out' in the next two years.

Quitting the Miracles

Despite these hits and a number of well-received albums (*Special Occasion, Time Out, Four In Blue* and *What Love Has Joined Together*, among others), Robinson's productivity was waning. He was preparing to leave the Miracles before the end of the decade when they accidentally accrued their biggest hit, 'Tears Of A Clown'. Taken from the LP *Make It Happen*, the song began life as an instrumental track created by Stevie Wonder and his producer, Hank Cosby, and was then brought to Smokey to add lyrics. The *Make It Happen* LP was dead for almost three years when Motown's London office took 'Tears Of A Clown' off the shelf for release as a single. Its rapid climb to Number 1 in Britain prompted Motown to follow suit in the US, where it also raced to the chart summit, in December 1970.

The turn of events obliged Smokey to delay his departure for a couple of years. He was only too aware that for Pete Moore, Bobby Rogers and Ronnie White, touring represented their most lucrative source of income. The quartet evenly divided record royalties, but none of the other members could match their leader's songwriting and publishing income. To ignore the demand for the Miracles that followed 'Tears Of A Clown' would have been unfair to his three friends and colleagues.

Robinson's delayed departure serves to illustrate the personal integrity and consideration for others that had been so typical of the man. There have been no tales of

tantrums in the studio or back-stage demonstrations of ego told by the artists with whom he has worked. And although he and Berry Gordy encountered prejudice and other setbacks during Motown's formative years, Robinson displays no grudge. Apparently in harmony with the world, he personifies his own lyrics: sensitive, compassionate, perceptive.

In January 1972, Smokey Robinson took the plunge, announcing that he would leave the Miracles that summer, after a nationwide 'farewell' tour. And leave he did, bowing out by way of *1957-1972*, a live album that contained a selection of the group's hits. He had many from which to choose: during the Miracles' 15 years together as a professional act, the group placed 39 singles on *Billboard*'s pop charts, including 15 which went Top Twenty and six which went Top Ten.

It is tempting to compare the success of Smokey with, and without, the Miracles, but it serves little purpose. His solo career was initially low-profile by design, yielding only three albums in as many years: *Smokey, Pure Smokey* and *A Quiet Storm*. He produced the first with Willie Hutch. It featured several revivals ('Will You Love Me Tomorrow', 'Never My Love', 'Never Can Say Goodbye') and two songs of particular note, 'Sweet Harmony', a touching tribute to the Miracles, and 'Just My Soul Responding', a rare venture into protest and social commentary.

Pure Smokey displayed a firmer grip on song content, as Robinson explored increasingly mature themes in songs such as 'It's Her Turn To Live', 'The Love Between Me And My Kids' and 'Virgin Man'. *A Quiet Storm* confirmed that he had hit his stride as a solo artist, exemplified by 'Baby That's Backatcha', a soul chart-topper and Top Thirty entry in the pop market.

Yet Robinson displayed no great desire to increase his recording output. With Willie Hutch, he began work on the music for a stage project, 'Cotillion', which was

ultimately abandoned. He dabbled in acting, appearing in episodes of television's 'Police Story' and 'Police Woman', then financed and produced the film entitled *Big Time*, for which he also scored the soundtrack. Movie and music sank without trace, losing Smokey a substantial amount of money.

Smokey in the charts

The most gratifying aspect of the man's solo career has come in the last few years, with two major hits that can be counted as the essence of Smokey: 'Cruisin'' (1979) and 'Being With You' (1981). The former originated as a Marv Tarplin riff (predating Motown's move to Los Angeles in 1972) though it took shape as a fully fledged song only on Robinson's 1979 album, *Where There's Smoke*. Rejecting that LP's first single, a disco retread of 'Get Ready', a radio station in Chicago began airing 'Cruisin'' – and found that the phones lit up with listener response. Similar reaction elsewhere eventually propelled the record to the Top Five of the US pop and R&B charts in early 1980.

The following year, when rock singer Kim Carnes secured a hit by reviving the Miracles' 'More Love', Robinson approached her producer, George Tobin, and played him a couple of new songs written for Carnes. 'I sure would like to record them on you,' responded Tobin. The result was 'Being With You', a crisp, clean, radio-oriented smash.

In the Eighties Smokey Robinson continued to sell records for the company he helped establish. After writing and producing dozens of hits since 1959 – to say nothing of the countless covers of his work, from the Beatles to the Beat, from the Rolling Stones to Linda Ronstadt, from Otis Redding to Deborah Harry – he still feels the thrill of hit records: 'I don't think anybody ever feels differently. I'm very, very blessed to have them after more than 20 years.'
ADAM WHITE

SMOKEY ROBINSON AND THE MIRACLES
Discography

Singles
Got A Job/My Mama Done Told Me (End 1016, 1958); I Cry/Money (End 1029, 1958); I Cry/Money (End 1084, 1960); Bad Girl/I Love You Baby (Motown 1/2, 1959); Bad Girl/I Love You Baby (Chess 1734, 1959); I Need A Change/All I Want (Chess 1769, 1960); Depend On Me/Way Over There (Tamla 54028, 1960); Shop Around/Who's Lovin' You (Tamla 54034, 1960); Ain't It, Baby/The Only One I Love (Tamla 54036, 1961); Broken Hearted/Mighty Good Loving (Tamla 54044, 1961); Everybody's Gotta Pay Some Dues/I Can't Believe (Tamla 54048, 1961); What's So Good About Good-Bye/I've Been Good To You (Tamla 54053, 1962); I'll Try Something New/You Never Miss A Good Thing (Tamla 54059, 1962); Way Over There/If Your Mother Only Knew (Tamla 54069, 1962); You've Really Got A Hold On Me/Happy Landing (Tamla 54073, 1962); A Love She Can Count On/I Can Take A Hint (Tamla 54078, 1963); Mickey's Monkey/Whatever Makes You Happy (Tamla 54083, 1963); I Gotta Dance To Keep From Crying/Such Is Love, Such Is Life (Tamla 54089, 1963); The Man In You/Heartbreak Road (Tamla 54092, 1964); I Like It Like That/You're So Fine And Sweet (Tamla 54098, 1964); That's What Love Is Made Of/Would I Love You (Tamla 54102, 1964); Come On Do The Jerk/Baby Don't You Go (Tamla 54109, 1964); Ooo Baby Baby/All That's Good (Tamla 54113, 1965); The Tracks Of My Tears/A Fork In The Road (Tamla 54118, 1965); Since You Won My Heart/My Girl Has Gone (Tamla 54123, 1965) Going To A Go-Go/Choosey Beggar (Tamla 54127, 1965); Whole Lot Of Shakin' In My Heart/Oh Be My Love (Tamla 54134, 1966); (Come Round Here) I'm The One You Need/Save Me (Tamla 54140, 1966); The Love I Saw In You Was Just A Mirage/Come Spy With Me (Tamla 54145, 1967); More Love/Swept For You Baby (Tamla 54142, 1967); I Second That Emotion/You Must Be Love (Tamla 54159, 1967); If You Can Want/When The Words From Your Heart Get Caught Up In Your Throat (Tamla 54162, 1968); Yester Love/Much Better Off (Tamla 54167, 1968); Special Occasion/ Give Her Up (Tamla 54172, 1968); Baby Baby Don't Cry/Your Mother's Only Daughter (Tamla 54178, 1969); Here I Go Again/Doggone Right (Tamla 54183, 1969); Abraham, Martin & John/Much Better Off (Tamla 54184, 1969); Darling Dear/Point It Out (Tamla 54189, 1969); Who's Gonna Take The Blame/I Gotta Thing For You (Tamla 54194, 1970); The Tears Of A Clown/Promise Me (Tamla 54199, 1970); That Girl/I Don't Blame You At All (Tamla 54205, 1971); Crazy About The La La La/Oh Baby Baby I Love You (Tamla 54206, 1971); Satisfaction/Flower Girl (Tamla 54211, 1971); We've Come Too Far To End It Now/When Sundown Comes (Tamla 54220, 1972); I Can't Stand To See You Cry/With Your Love Came (Tamla 54225, 1972); Sweet Harmony/Want To Know My Mind (Tamla 54233, 1973); Don't Let It End/Wigs And Washes (Tamla 54237, 1973); Baby Come Close/A Silent Partner In A 3 Way Love Affair (Tamla 54239, 1973); Give Me Just Another Day/I Wanna Be With You (Tamla 5420, 1973); It's Her Turn To Live/Just My Soul Responding (Tamla 54248, 1974); Do It Baby/I Wanna Be With You (Tamla 54248, 1974); Virgin Man/Fulfill Your Need (Tamla 54250, 1974); I Am, I Am/The Family Sung (Tamla 54251, 1974); Don't Cha Love It/Up Again (Tamla 54256, 1974); Baby That's Backatcha/Just Passing Through (Tamla 54258, 1975); You Are Love/Gemini (Tamla 54259, 1975); The Agony And The Ecstasy/The Wedding Song (Tamla 54261, 1975); Love Machine Pt 1/Love Machine Pt 2 (Tamla 54262, 1975); Asleep On My Love/Quiet Storm (Tamla 54265, 1976); Open/Coincidentally (Tamla 54267, 1976); Night Life/Smog (Tamla 54268, 1976); When You Came/Coincidentally (Tamla 54269, 1976); Old Fashioned Man/Just Passing Through (Tamla 54276, 1976); Humming Song/There Will Come A Day (Tamla 54279, 1977); Vitamin U/Holly (Tamla 54284, 1977); Theme From Big Time Pt 1/Theme From Big Time Pt 2 (Tamla 54288, 1977); Why Don't You Wanna See My Bad Side/Daylight And Darkness (Tamla 54293, 1978); I'm Loving You Softly/Shoe Soul (Tamla 54296, 1978); Ever Had A Dream/Get Ready (Tamla 54301, 1979); Cruisin'/Ever Had A Dream (Tamla 54306, 1979); Let Me Be The Clock/Travelin' Through (Tamla 54311, 1980); Heavy On Pride (Light On Love)/I Love The Nearness of You (Tamla 54313, 1980); I Want To Be Your Love/Wine, Women And Song (Tamla 54318, 1980); Being With You/What's In Your Life For Me (Tamla 54321, 1981); You Are Forever/I Hear The Children Singing (Tamla 54327, 1981); So Sad/Food For Thought (Tamla 54332, 1981); Tell Me Tomorrow Pt 1/Tell Me Tomorrow Pt 2 (Tamla 1601, 1981).

Albums (selective)
Hi-We're The Miracles (Tamla 220); *Shop Around* (Tamla 224); *Cookin'* (Tamla 223); *Doin' Mickey's Monkey* (Tamla 245); *Going To A Go-Go* (Tamla 267); *Tears Of A Clown* (Tamla 276); *A Pocket Full Of Miracles* (Tamla 306); *One Dozen Roses* (Tamla 312).

SAX 'N' SOUL

The tough rhythm and blues of Junior Walker

JUNIOR WALKER (christened Autry De-Walt) was born into a Baptist family in Blytheville, Arkansas, in 1938. In 1958 he moved north to Chicago, eventually settling in nearby South Bend, Indiana, where his interest in alto and tenor sax was stimulated by seeing a well-known local musician, George Mason. Soon Autry was investigating players like Gene Ammons, Louis Jordan, Earl Bostic and Illinois Jacquet. Above all he revered the ferocious bop of Charlie Parker and the gutbucket style of Nashville sessionman Homer 'Boots' Randolph. After he became proficient on a saxophone loaned to him by his uncle, his mother bought him an instrument of his own and his career was launched.

In 1953, while still at high school, he formed the Jumping Jacks with guitarist Willie Woods and adopted the stage name Junior Walker. (Apocryphal stories abound concerning this name – most of them from his own lips. Sometimes he attributes it to his boyhood habit of walking just about anywhere, no matter how far; sometimes he mentions a stepfather and shrugs.) With the inclusion of drummer Billy 'Sticks' Nix, they became the Sticks Nix Band and played dates in the locality, consolidating interest throughout the region.

By the late Fifties the group was based in Battle Creek, Michigan; Walker led a line-up that consisted of Woods, Ray Free-man (guitar), plus local acquisitions Jimmy Graves (guitar), Victor Thomas (organ) and Tony Washington (drums). Freeman and Graves were virtually interchangeable, floating members of a band that functioned mostly as a quartet. The group's ability to play almost anything on request rapidly earned them the name 'All Stars'.

Detroit connections

A chance meeting with fellow Southerner Johnny Bristol in a small club in Battle Creek resulted in Junior Walker and the All Stars backing Johnny and Jack Beavers in Detroit. Gwen Gordy (sister of Tamla boss Berry Gordy) spotted the duo and introduced them to her husband Harvey Fuqua, former bass singer with the Moonglows. He signed them to his Anna-Tri-Phi label where they promptly cut 'Do You See My Love'. (Curiously enough it provided Junior with a Number 32 Hot Hundred hit when his version was released years later in 1970!) Back in 1962, it was Johnny Bristol who persuaded Fuqua to produce Junior for his Harvey label. The first single, 'Twist Lackawanna', merely suggested that the All Stars were an ebullient dance combo, but the follow-up, 'Cleo's Mood', issued in February 1963, was a better indication of their quality. This piece of blues balladry allowed Junior to show his abrasive sax sound for the first time. By now Fuqua was well pleased with his acquisition and, after one more single, 'Good Rockin'', he sold up and took Junior with him to Motown late in 1963.

For nearly 12 months the All Stars honed their skills on the chitterling circuit, testing numbers like 'Monkey Jump' and 'Satan's Blues' before unleashing these two sides as their debut single on Motown's subsidiary Soul label. Their second release for Soul, the Junior Walker composition 'Shotgun', established them nationwide. In a matter of weeks this vicious jolt of R&B, featuring Junior's manic horn over slithery organ, blasted its way to Number 4 in the US charts in March 1965. Quite the equal of anything laid down by King Curtis or Booker T. and the MGs, it set the tone for Junior's best work over the next three years. With the smell of success in his nostrils he quickly issued another dance-crazed opus, 'Do The Boomerang', in May 1965 which scythed to Number 36 in the Hot Hundred.

Next came the moody 'Cleo's Back', a Willie Woods tune produced by Harvey Fuqua, coupled with the priceless 'Shake And Fingerpop'. The latter was a frenetic celebration of the barracuda dance, although according to Junior he had no particular dance in mind, only the mood of the moment. The next single, the infectious 'Road Runner', with its torrid flipside 'Shoot Your Shot', peaked at Number 20 nationally in 1966. For most afficionados it remains one of the Motown master sounds, an all-time floor filler with Junior sweating up a storm and squealing like a stuck pig. The redoubtable team of Holland-Dozier-Holland wrote and produced the song. In the UK it found favour as late as April 1969 when it made Number 12 in the charts.

Red-hot R&B continued to flow with 'Baby You Know It Ain't Right', 'How Sweet It Is', 'Money', 'Pucker Up Buttercup', 'Hip City' and 'Home Cookin''. The best sides, particularly 'How Sweet It Is' and 'Hip City', crackled with life and suggested that the All Stars were jamming at some riotous houseparty rather than in some dark studio corner. The same seeming spontaneity – no doubt the legacy of working so many clubs – informed the first three albums, *Shotgun* (1965), *Soul Session* and *Road Runner* (both 1966).

Unfortunately the ascendancy of uptown soul in the late Sixties forced Junior to dilute his style in order to survive. Once again Johnny Bristol, now a fully fledged writer and producer, was waiting to help him on his way. Strings, polite vocals and heavy choral support were the order of the day. Junior resisted recording 'What Does It Take' for nearly two years until Bristol finally persuaded him. Concealed on the *Home Cookin'* album of 1968, it found favour with disc jockeys and was released as a single. It made Number 4 and 13 in the US and UK pop charts in the following year, and the die was cast for future releases. Similar confections followed fast and included 'These Eyes', 'Gotta Hold On To This Feeling' and 'Take Me Girl I'm Ready'. Of the releases of the early Seventies, only 'Way Back Home' and perhaps 'Walk In The Night', which reached Number 16 in the UK in 1972, had merit.

'Way Back Home' was an outstanding tune originally written by Wilton Felder for the Crusaders with brilliantly evocative lyrics from Johnny Bristol and Gladys Knight. The song gave Junior his last indisputable classic.

Junior Walker had always sensed his limitations as a singer and after 'Groove Thang' in the summer of 1972, when his liaison with Briston ended, he returned instinctively, if briefly, to mainstream R&B. His own production, 'Gimme That Beat', released in January 1973, welded the hard-blowing sound of his heyday to the vocal raunch of James Brown. Sales were negligible but the record wasn't. The real problem was that Junior had become an anachronism in the supposedly sophisticated world of jazz-funk. A move to Los Angeles in 1976 and a change of label to Whitfield in 1979 made little difference.

Walker would never begrudge people their success, and about current trends he remains phlegmatic: 'It's the same thing. You sell a car, you sell a Ford, then change it to something else. The beat is just heavier. I been playing it all my life.'   CLIVE ANDERSON

Junior Walker: a tough singer (left) and a raunchy saxophonist (right). Below: Junior with the All Stars.

Junior Walker
Recommended Listening

Junior Walker's Greatest Hits (Tamla Motown STML 11120) (Includes: Shotgun, How Sweet It Is, Road Runner, Hip City, Shoot Your Shot, Pucker Up Buttercup, What Does It Take, Shake And Fingerpop, Home Cookin').

What's Going On?

Marvin Gaye: from pop star to black progressive

In 1980, MARVIN GAYE arrived in London – on the run from bankruptcy, two broken marriages and the Motown organisation of which he had been such a central part for 20 years. The impasse which Gaye appeared to have reached in his life was evident from the concerts he performed at that time. For the most part they were the performances of a distracted and troubled man, with Gaye playing the part of a stage lotario almost to the lengths of self-parody, fumbling the lyrics to his songs and threatening, it was said, to fire his band before, during and after almost every show. And yet there was still evidence of Gaye's consummate prowess as a singer, the relaxed sensuality of his performance, and an almost palpable air of penitence and sorrow beneath the braggadocio. It was as if Gaye himself was aware that all this was a charade of no great importance, merely a temporary respite from the deep but unspecified concerns which now dominated his life.

If the impression Gaye gave at this time was of an artist fettered by troubles of unfathomable complexity, the picture which had emerged in his early and formative years with Motown could not have been more different. The hits which took Marvin Gaye through the Sixties showed not a care in the world. He, after all, was the Crown Prince of Motown: suave, lean, cool and ineffably charming.

While Smokey Robinson's pliant, yielding soprano cast him as the hapless romantic in his songs, Gaye – with his light, airy yet discreetly arrogant delivery and wolfish smile – *broke hearts*, even when he sang of his own being broken.

Church echoes

Marvin Gaye was born in Washington on 2 April 1939, the son of a church minister. As a young boy he sang and played organ in the church choir, but he was, by his own admission, a difficult child 'with a natural aversion to authority and regimentation'. At the age of 16 he enlisted under age in the United States Air Force, believing that he would be drafted into the Special Air Services. Instead, Gaye found himself pumping fuel into aeroplanes, and subsequently waged a personal war of attrition against the airforce which resulted in him being discharged.

Returning to Washington, Gaye began to sing with various local groups. He joined Don Covay and Billy Stewart for personal appearances in a group called the Rainbows, and recorded briefly for the Okeh label with the Marquees, before being invited to join the Moonglows, a celebrated doo-wop group, then in a second incarnation under the direction of Harvey Fuqua. Gaye recorded with the Moonglows for Chess, but the re-formation was short-lived. When Fuqua moved to Detroit with his wife Gwendoline Gordy, Gaye came too, marrying Gwen's sister Anna. With the assistance of his old employers Leonard and Phil Chess, Fuqua set up Anna-Tri-Phi Records with his wife; one of the first releases on the label was a song called 'Money', written by Janie Bradford and Berry Gordy. Soon afterwards, the Anna label and Berry Gordy's Tamla affiliated, with Gaye joining Tamla as a solo singer.

At first, Gaye doubled with Tamla as a session drummer, playing on the early Miracles records and Stevie Wonder's 1963 hit 'Fingertips'. His first solo release on the label was 'Let Your Conscience Be Your Guide', a song written and produced by Berry Gordy and released in the US in May 1961. This was well before Motown records had gelled into a definable sound, and Gaye's earliest records intimated a sense of rugged spontaneity that was closer to his gospel roots than to the smooth soul for which he would later become renowned. 'Stubborn Kind of Fellow' and 'Hitch Hike', featuring vocal backing by the Vandellas – for whom Gaye was to co-write 'Dancing In The Street', their 1964 smash – gave the singer his first American hits in 1962 and 1963 respectively. His early style reached its apotheosis later in 1963 with 'Pride and Joy' and 'Can I Get A Witness' – the latter a roistering, uninhibited gospel work-out driven along by handclaps, tambourines, strident piano chords and a call-and-response choir. Motown would never get as close to church again, while the Rolling Stones' cover of the song on their first album brought Gaye to the notice of a wider, white audience.

Seven-day weeks

Gaye maintained a somewhat unusual position in Motown in these early years. He was a member of the Motortown Revue, touring by bus and working mostly halls and record-hops. The wage of 200 dollars for a 7-day week was well earned; when the Revue played a theatre like the Apollo in Harlem, up to six or seven shows were packed into a single day. As Gordy's brother-in-law, Gaye was assured of his position as a member of the Motown 'family', but – like all his fellow-acts – his career was shaped by the atmosphere of rivalry as well as support which dominated the company.

Berry Gordy's policy of 'selective marketing' – releasing only those records that were deemed chart certainties, and concentrating on breaking only two or three acts at a time – had producers and

Right: Marvin Gaye basks in the limelight at the Albert Hall in 1976. Far right: The singer early in his career. Insets, left to right: The women singers he worked with during his career – Florence Lyles, Kim Weston and Tammi Terrell.

writers vying with each other to work with the acts most favoured by Gordy. From 1964 onwards, the dominance of the Supremes and the Four Tops left the other artists anxiously awaiting the nod from the inner sanctum that could mean the difference between stardom and anonymity.

Gaye had a unique advantage, however; by his own admission 'a spoilt brat', he could use his family connections when he didn't get on with producers or writers – which was often. Gaye seemingly worked with almost every producer on the Motown books at one time or another, being teamed with Gordy himself, then William Stevenson, Holland, Dozier and Holland and then Smokey Robinson; the latter's soaring, deceptively easy melodies and sweetly-driving production were particularly suited to Gaye's eminently relaxed vocal style on the 1965 hits 'I'll Be Doggone' and 'Ain't That Peculiar'.

This may have been to Gaye's advantage; certainly, he never grew dependent on one producer, as happened to Martha and the Vandellas and the Four Tops, who suffered when Holland, Dozier and Holland left Motown. Instead, Gaye's talent was stretched and extended in various settings across the years, from the sly, jazz-influenced styling of Berry Gordy's 'Try It Baby' in 1964 to the dark, voodoo mystery of the million-selling 'I Heard It Through The Grapevine' in 1968 – a Number 1 on both sides of the Atlantic and showpiece for Norman Whitfield's startlingly melodramatic production. Although it had already been recorded by Gladys Knight and taken to the Number 2 position in the Hot Hundred, it is Gaye's version which is more often remembered.

Gaye's good looks and easy charm brought him a sizeable female audience

and led him to be paired over the years with a number of the label's girl singers. He first recorded with Mary Wells in 1964, then Kim Weston (with whom he made 'It Takes Two' – a particular dance-floor favourite in the UK), and in later years he would join forces with Diana Ross. But unquestionably the sweetest partnership of all was that of Gaye and Tammi Terrell. That began in 1967 with the delightful 'Ain't No Mountain High Enough', establishing a singular rapport between the two singers and the songs of a young husband-and-wife songwriting and production team, Nickolas Ashford and Valerie Simpson.

Ashford and Simpson's songs were perfect romantic vignettes, constructed with Swiss-watch precision, and their productions on hits like 'Ain't Nothing Like The Real Thing' and 'You're All I Need To Get By' were absolute masterpieces – luscious, heartfelt and touching. Gaye's chart partnership with Terrell lasted on an off for the three years from 1967 to 1969 and it was as if it brought out in Gaye a heightening of the sensitivity in his performance. On record, at least, it was the perfect love affair, but its ending was to be desperately tragic. In 1969, Terrell collapsed on stage in Gaye's arms; after some months and innumerable operations she finally died in 1970 from complications resulting from a brain tumour.

Love on the rocks

Gaye was devastated. He ceased touring altogether and went into seclusion. Personally and professionally his life was drifting onto the rocks: his marriage to Anna

was under strain, relations with Berry Gordy were wearing thin and record sales were tailing off perceptibly. It was clear that Gaye was no longer responding to the dictates of Motown's autocratic system.

But that, too, was undergoing profound change. Having experienced eight years of explosive growth, Motown were now subject to pressures from within and without. Many of the label's original hitmakers had fallen by the wayside or, realising the total control the label exercised over their careers, had moved elsewhere. The United States, too, was in turmoil, gripped by a popular feeling against the war in Vietnam, hung-over from student protest and inner-city riots which even Motown –

Marvin Gaye
Recommended Listening

The Hits of Marvin Gaye (Tamla Motown STML 11201) (Includes: I Heard It Through The Grapevine, Abraham, Martin and John, What's Going On, Inner City Blues, How Sweet It Is, Mercy, Mercy Me, Too Busy Thinking About My Baby). *What's Going On* Tamla Motown STML 11190) (Includes: What's Happening Brother, What's Going On, Save The Children). *In Our Lifetime* (Motown STML 12149). *Let's Get It On* (Tamla Motown STMS 5034) (Please Don't Stay, Let's Get It On, If I Should Die Tonight, Keep Gettin' It On, Come Get To This, Distant Lover, You Sure Love To Ball, Just To Keep You Satisfied).

decamping now to the safer climes of Los Angeles – could not afford to ignore.

In this period of uncertainty and flux, Gaye began working as writer, arranger and producer on a new project, a concept album that would capture the spirit of the age – anti-war, pro-ecology, a hymn to the unity of the people. Gaye saw it as the record that would establish him as a great artist, not simply a pawn of the Motown machine. The resulting album, *What's Going On*, was completed at the end of 1970. Berry Gordy and the other Motown executives listened to it in shocked disbelief. But Gaye prevailed: release it, or I go. Motown relented, and in the beginning of 1971 the record finally saw release.

What's Going On was, on all fronts, the masterpiece Gaye had believed it to be. Musically, he had in one fell swoop taken black music into virgin terrain, building on the sweetness and drama of Motown's established production techniques with rich orchestrations and arrangements that brought a new depth and mystery to the music. The concerns of the songs catalysed the development of a social conscience in black music, which was to surface so visibly in the work of Curtis Mayfield, and the songs of Gamble and Huff. For Gaye himself, the brooding, meditative quality of *What's Going On*, the tone of plangent melancholia of his performance showed him to be a changed man.

Contrary to Motown's fears, *What's Going On* re-established Gaye in the charts with a vengeance. The album reached the US Top Ten and yielded three million-selling singles in the title track, 'Mercy, Mercy Me' and 'Inner City Blues'. For the first time, an artist had called Motown's bluff, and Gaye's success was to have widespread repercussions within the label – most notably with Stevie Wonder. The freedom thus achieved was to result in *Music Of My Mind* and subsequent musical landmarks from Wonder later in the decade. For Motown, it meant a belated recognition of the album market which had been opened up in the late Sixties by white rock performers and their record companies; thenceforth, albums would consist of more than two or three singles among filler material.

For Gaye himself, the pattern had been set for his future work. The film soundtrack *Trouble Man* was more successful than the movie for which it was written, while 1973's *Let's Get It On* was nothing less than an exercise in steamy eroticism. The singer co-wrote and produced every track to confirm a total all-round success. The album's intended sequel, *I Want You*, appeared in 1976; it was inevitably an anti-climax, and much of the material had been written by Leon Ware and other

In the face of broken marriages and artistic battles with Motown in the Seventies, Gaye (left) became preoccupied with spiritual matters. Opposite: Gaye in the Eighties – sadder but wiser?

outside contributors. The social concerns which had so preoccupied Gaye in the early Seventies seemed to have blissfully evaporated.

Back to the stage
Gaye had returned to the concert stage after an absence of nearly six years in 1974, and his first appearance at the Oakland-Alameda County Coliseum was captured on the *Marvin Gaye Live* album. A further live set of more modern material, recorded at the London Palladium, surfaced in 1977, with one side of the double album occupied by the 10-minute plus 'Got To Give It Up'. A studio-recorded disco track built around a repetitive riff, it was a marked change of style for Gaye from his laid-back Seventies output thus far; released as a single, it reached the top of the US charts and made Number 7 in the UK at the height of the disco boom.

Other big hits had been lifted from the *Diana And Marvin* album of 1974 in 'You Are Everything' and 'Stop Look Listen (To Your Heart)'. Although they broke no new musical ground – both were easy-listening covers of Stylistics hits – they nevertheless found Marvin and Diana (Ross) in fine vocal form and were substantial UK successes at Numbers 5 and 25 respectively.

Marvin Gaye's records appeared to suggest a man who had slipped into a state of contented and constant exercise of his libido; but his personal and professional life was clearly in some disarray. The gaps between recordings grew longer, his stage appearances intermittent; he shaved his head, embraced overt spirituality and his marriage ended in a painful and public divorce. The record which chronicled this latter development with unflinching honesty was *Here, My Dear*. Released in 1978, it struck a remarkable balance between poignancy and bitterness, reflecting on the mixed blessings of marriage and bemoaning the iniquities of the alimony arrangements.

The singer's life appeared to be in a shambles. He remarried soon afterwards, but that, too, quickly ended in divorce; he received a demand for taxes close to two million dollars and declared bankruptcy. Gaye left Los Angeles and moved to Hawaii, and from there to London, where he attempted to stitch his life back together again with a round of live performances and the release, in 1981, of his first album in three years, *In Our Lifetime*.

For Gaye, the album was very much a compromise. He had planned an album which articulated his increasing obsession with spiritual matters – a record which would delineate the conflict between good and evil – a pronouncement for the Eighties as *What's Going On* had been for the Seventies. But once again, Motown intervened. What resulted was half the album Gaye had wanted to make, and half tracks which he had recorded earlier for an aborted project called *Love Man*. Gaye himself was disappointed with the album's content, and its sound, which he thought 'too Motown'.

After long standing problems with Gordy, Gaye left the label in 1981 for Columbia Records, who issued his fantastically successful album, *Midnight Love*, and hit single, 'Sexual Healing', in 1982.

His career was taking an upward turn again, but his life ended tragically on 1 April 1984, the eve of his 45th birthday, when Marvin Gaye was shot twice through the chest during an argument with his clergyman father, aged 70, who was later charged. Gaye Snr claimed he had acted in self-defence when his son, high on drugs, began attacking him.
MICK BROWN

How Motown's superstar spread her wings

BERRY GORDY JR has been a shrewd decision-maker many times in his life, but never more so than when he planned the departure of Diana Ross from the Supremes. He knew then, in the late Sixties, that Motown Records would evolve into the multi-media entertainment complex of his ambitions only if it had a multi-media superstar – one who could capture the public imagination, and its disposable income, through sheer intensity of talent, personality and style.

He wanted Ross to be that superstar. He wanted her to join that 'rarified constellation of first-name acceptance alongside Barbra, Billie, Ella and Judy'. Indeed, that quote itself – from one of Motown's 1970 trade press advertisements – revealed Gordy's interest in the performer through whom he hoped Ross could secure 'first-name acceptance': Billie Holiday. So it was no surprise when, twelve months later, Motown announced that the former Supreme would make her motion-picture debut in a biography of the late jazz singer entitled *Lady Sings The Blues* (1972).

Truth is no stranger

In fact, much of Ross's own career in the Seventies might have been scripted for a movie: the challenge of her first solo appearances ('Welcome to the can-Diana-Ross-make-it-on-her-own show', the singer said on opening night); the intimate relationship, professional and personal, with Berry Gordy; and her subsequent controversial marriage to a white man. Her music, too, reinforced the Hollywood connection. Recordings like 'Reach Out And Touch', 'Ain't No Mountain High Enough', 'Touch Me In The Morning' and 'Love Hangover' were passionate, big-production adventures in the sonic equivalent of CinemaScope.

As one of Berry Gordy's executives said in 1973: 'The record artists of Motown have built great public identification, which is almost exactly like the old Hollywood "star quality".' He might have said 'star system', because Gordy appeared to be pursuing his new goals with all the arrogance and autocracy of the old-time movie moguls. When Paramount Pictures, with whom Motown made *Lady Sings The Blues*, baulked at some aspects of the production, Gordy paid the studio two million dollars for creative control of the finished film. On a later occasion, when Tony Richardson, the director of *Mahogany* (1975), disagreed with Gordy over certain creative elements of that movie, the Motown boss fired him and became the director himself.

Ross didn't always go along with the game plan of her mentor. Gordy, for example, didn't want to release 'Reach Out And Touch' as her first solo single in 1970, because it was a waltz and totally unlike the music that her fans were used to hearing. But the singer felt strongly about the song's message, particularly in the light of the social alienation of the times brought about by the Vietnam War.

The give-and-take between Gordy and Ross was probably at the heart of her rise to superstardom in the Seventies. The first couple of solo years were concerned with the media by which she had previously established her popularity: records, concerts and television. Her live appearances collected good reviews, especially at New York's Waldorf Astoria and Hollywood's Coconut Grove, and if tickets were beyond the financial means of most Supremes fans, Diana's discs provided an acceptable substitute. Her first and third albums, released in 1970 and 1971 respectively, *Diana Ross* and *Surrender* (entitled *I'm Still Waiting* in Britain), were among her best.

Much of the material was written and produced by Nick Ashford and Valerie Simpson, who recognised that the singer's finest – and most commercial – music came from a carefully crafted combination of melodrama and vulnerability. Those qualities were evident in 'Ain't No Mountain High Enough', which swept to the top of the US charts in September 1970, and in 'Remember Me', which followed it into the Top Twenty four months later. 'I'm Still Waiting', poignantly penned and produced by Deke Richards, reached the summit in Britain during August 1971, Diana's only UK chart-topper of the decade.

Diana's mid-Seventies image of feline sensuality and million-dollar sophistication was both beguiling and exclusive.

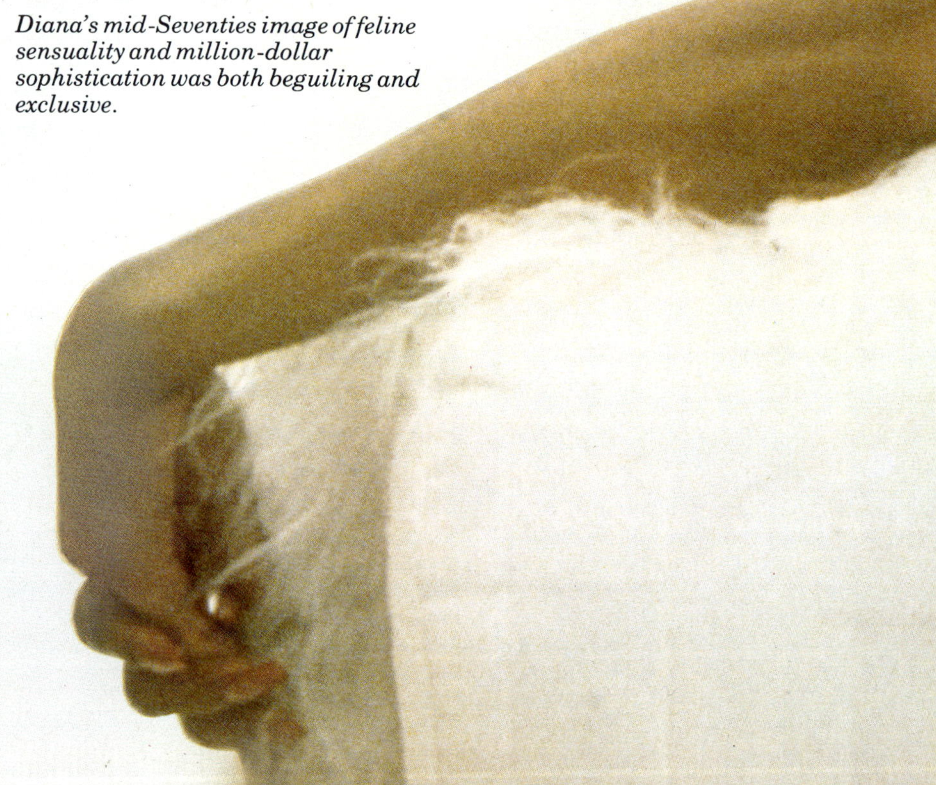

In 1972, Gordy's plans for Hollywood stardom for Ross began to take shape when she began filming *Lady Sings The Blues*. It was a consuming experience, by all accounts. She plunged herself into the role, researching and absorbing every aspect, every detail of Billie Holiday's tempestuous, tragic life and death. 'I read anything anyone had written about her,' said Ross. 'I went to the library, read newspaper clippings, the backs of album covers. I got pictures from her personal collection and studied them, everything from her red fingernails to the knick-knacks on the table. And as I went to sleep at night, I'd try to imagine how Billie Holiday would feel going to sleep after a hard day's work.'

The finished movie reflected both Diana's commitment to the role and her innate acting ability – much to the surprise of critics who, while castigating the script's misrepresentations of Holiday's life, acknowledged that Ross had captured the singer's spirit, her essence. For once, a publicity catchphrase ('Diana Ross *is* Billie Holiday') was not merely movie-makers' hype.

Lady Sings The Blues was a hit, generating close to 20 million dollars at the box-office in North America alone, as well as a Number 1 soundtrack package of such Holiday classics as 'God Bless The Child', 'Good Morning Heartache' (also a Top Forty single in the US in 1973) and 'T'ain't Nobody's Bizness If I Do'. Recognition for Diana personally came in the form of an Oscar nomination for best actress. She didn't win, but later observed, graciously, 'It showed any little black girl living in Detroit's Brewster project who watched TV that night that she, too, can be up there one day.'

On the sentimental side

For all that she had given to Gordy and to *Lady Sings The Blues*, Ross took care of some personal business during 1971-72. She married publicist Bob Silberstein, and gave birth to daughters Rhonda and Tracee (a third child, Chudney, was born a couple of years later). It was surprising not for the fact of black marrying white, but that Ross should marry anyone but Berry Gordy. Their intimacy throughout the Supremes' heyday was well-publicised, to the point where Gordy once admitted that he had 'tried to marry her a couple of times'. Then he said, 'Why should she marry me when she's got me already?'

But if Diana Ross was achieving goals in acting and in her personal affairs, her music was becoming less than satisfying. 'Touch Me In The Morning', a dramatic ballad, was a major hit, but the subsequent album of the same name, released in 1973, carried that song's underlying sentimentality too far, featuring cloying covers of songs such as the Carpenters' 'I Won't Last A Day Without You' and John Lennon's 'Imagine'. The decline was only partially arrested by *Diana And Marvin* (1974), a comfortable (and occasionally seductive) union with Motown's premier male singer, Marvin Gaye. It yielded several hits, despite the fact that it was rumoured that the two singers were never in the recording studio at the same time.

These and other LPs exemplified the problems of Diana on disc between 1973 and 1978. She allowed herself to be recorded by any number of producers – Michael Masser, Tom Baird, Michael Randall, Mel Larson and Jerry Marcellino, Hal Davis, Ron Miller, Bob Gaudio – so that each album became a patchwork quilt of different moods and styles, often lacking conviction. What had been tolerable in the singles-oriented Sixties was no longer the case, especially after the satisfying nature of Ross' initial solo work with Ashford and Simpson. The Richard Perry-produced *Baby It's Me* in 1977 was an attempt to correct this situation that was, sadly, a creative disappointment.

By contrast, Diana Ross in concert was almost always confident and convincing. Her shows were extravaganzas – theatrical and showbiz-heavy, featuring Broadway tunes and Tin Pan Alley standards – but never dull. Her 1976 world tour, staged as 'An Evening With Diana Ross' and subsequently issued as a live album in 1977, exhibited her enthusiasm and inter-reaction with her audience. Many of the songs seemed like personal statements, even the somewhat earnest tribute to 'the working girls' (Billie Holiday, Josephine Baker, Ethel Waters, Bessie Smith). And if Ross rather rushed through the Supremes segment, most fans forgave her in face of the show's sheer spectacle.

For Diana's second movie, Berry Gordy chose a more conventional vehicle than *Lady Sings The Blues*. *Mahogany* was originally to have been a musical scored by B. B. Merrill, the composer of Streisand's *Funny Girl*, but it came out as straight drama, the tale of a jetsetting model's progress through the world of international

fashion. Cinematic clichés abounded, including the slogan coined by Gordy for the picture's publicity campaign: 'Success is nothing without someone you love to share it with.'

Mahogany was poorly received by the critics upon release in 1975, but generated more than 14 million dollars' worth of ticket sales. Diana Ross's performance of the title tune, a squishy ballad from the pens of Michael Masser and Gerry Goffin, topped the US charts and made Number 5 in the UK.

Commercial good fortune did not attend Diana's third movie, a mega-budget version of *The Wiz*, the Broadway hit musical based on *The Wizard Of Oz* to which Motown acquired rights in 1976. Universal Pictures was said to have spent more than 30 million dollars on producing the film – which also starred Richard Pryor, Lena Horne and Michael Jackson – only to watch it disappear into box-office oblivion. 1976 also saw her divorce – on account of 'irreconcilable differences' – from Robert Silberstein.

Out on her own

And so it was that Diana returned to records. She worked again with Nick Ashford and Valerie Simpson on *The Boss* (1979), an album of good songs and slick production, performed with panache and self-confidence. It was followed by an inspired union with Chic's Nile Rodgers and Bernard Edwards, whose street-smart, stripped-down songwriting and production techniques were then at the cutting edge of contemporary black music. *Diana* (1980) became her biggest-selling LP in eight years, spending a full 52 weeks on the *Billboard* charts and yielding the hit singles 'Upside Down', 'I'm Coming Out' and, in the UK, 'My Old Piano'.

Diana Ross left Motown early in 1981, just before her swansong for the label, 'Endless Love' with Lionel Richie, turned

Three facets of Diana Ross's towering performing talent – the smiling public relations woman (above left), the accomplished actress of Lady Sings The Blues *(above) and the entertainer (below).*

into an international smash. The departure was 'a business decision', she said at the time, emphasising that there were no 'problems' or disputes with the company or people who had helped her reach and retain superstardom. 'Motown is my family,' she stated. 'They always will be.'

The early Eighties saw Ross enjoying new freedom and control over her future. Her recording deal with RCA (for North America) and EMI (for the rest of the world) allowed her to produce her own albums, *Why Do Fools Fall In Love* (1981) and *Silk Electric* (1982), for the first time; she also began to write more of her own material. However, Diana continued to pay tribute to the man to whom she owed so much: 'I know that every day, if I have some decision to make about something, I think about what Berry Gordy would do. I want him to know this. I want him to know the effect he has on my life, and will always have on my life.'

ADAM WHITE

Diana Ross
Recommended Listening

Diana (Motown STMA8033) (Includes: I'm Coming Out, Upside Down, My Old Piano, Friend To Friend, Give Up); *Why Do Fools Fall In Love* (Capitol EST 26733) (Includes: Mirror Mirror, Why Do Fools Fall In Love, Endless Love, Work That Body, Never Too Late).

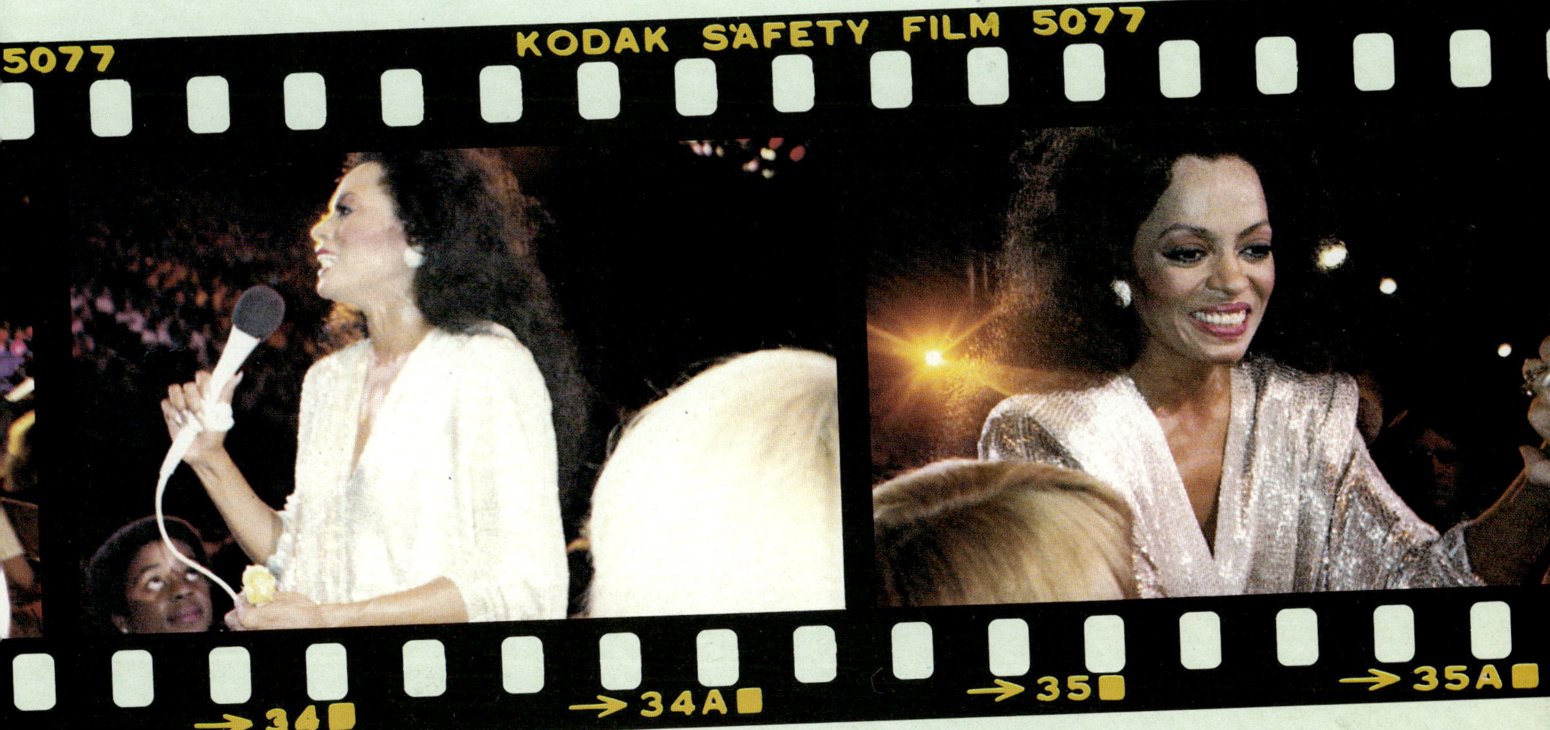

INNERVISIONS

Sweet sounds and insight from Stevie Wonder

IT IS LIKELY that with modern medical technology Steveland Morris would never have been blind. As it was, on 13 May 1950, too much oxygen found its way into two incubators in a hospital in Saginaw, Michigan; in one a girl died, while in the other the month-premature Stevie survived, but lost his sight.

The mother, Lula Hardaway, had already had two healthy children, Milton and Calvin, and while her youngest son's handicap was unexpected, she did her best to bring him up the same way as his elder brothers. Stevie's father, however, could not accept the burden, and eventually left the family.

As with most blind people, Stevie's other senses compensated for his lack of sight – in particular his hearing. Friendly neighbours would toss coins onto the kitchen table, and those that Stevie correctly guessed he kept. 'I could almost always get it right, except a penny and a nickel confused me.'

By the time he was four, Stevie's family had moved to Detroit in search of a better life. They settled, though, in Breckenridge, on the East side of the city – one of the worse slums – with most of its inhabitants working for the Ford Motor Company and the kids always in trouble. Stevie's interest in music was aroused by listening to radio station WCHB, on which he heard various R&B singers, including Johnny Ace. Other early influences included Little Walter, Jimmy Reed, the Coasters and Nat 'King' Cole.

After enduring all manner of pots and pans being banged all year round, his family found Christmas presents easy to buy for Stevie: toy drums, which, by Boxing Day, were invariably smashed to bits. Eventually a friendly barber gave him a four-holed harmonica on a chain, and an uncle later gave him a Hohner. His musical development was further assisted at the age of seven by two further gifts: a neighbour leaving the West side housing project where the family now lived left him her piano, while the local Lions club gave him a decent set of drums one Christmas.

Kerbside audition

Word of Stevie's talent soon spread further afield. Ron White, a member of Motown's successful group the Miracles, had heard his brother Gerald talk glowingly of the little blind boy, and went to hear him play. Suitably impressed by the multi-talented 11-year-old, White arranged to take him to Motown's studios the next day and introduce him to Brian Holland. As Brian was busy doing a session at the time, Stevie's

Little Stevie Wonder in the shade. Unlike many a child prodigy in rock, Wonder transcended record company hyperbole and public adulation to prove an enduring performer.

'audition' took place on the kerb of Woodward Boulevard.

After founder Berry Gordy had heard Stevie play, the company offered him a contract. As a minor, Stevie was not old enough to negotiate or sign for himself, so an official from the State of Michigan was appointed to make sure his contract guaranteed time for tutoring, that he wouldn't work long hours and that he was protected from the vices associated with the music world.

Little success

Stevie's friendliness, unspoilt nature and energetic love for his craft did not readily convert into healthy record sales: 'I Call It Pretty Music' (with Marvin Gaye on drums), 'Waterboy' (a duet with Clarence Paul) and 'Contract On Love' all failed to sell in quantity, giving Berry Gordy a problem. Motown was still in its infancy and could not subsidise singles failures indefinitely; it was obvious that Gordy needed a new image for his young charge.

Somewhere along the way, Steveland Morris had become Little Stevie Wonder: he wasn't yet in his teens, which accounted for the 'Little', and the staff and producers at Motown had taken to calling him 'the Boy Wonder'. Although there is some dispute as to who finally put the name together, by early June 1963 everyone in the United States knew who Little Stevie Wonder was. Berry Gordy had made his decision – since Stevie's charm transmitted perfectly during live performance, then why not put out a live record? It didn't matter that the song Gordy had chosen, 'Fingertips', was too long; he would simply chop it in half and promote the second side as 'Fingertips Part II'.

This decision proved to be a masterstroke; in barely six weeks, the single was Number 1 in the Hot Hundred (one week after it had topped the R&B charts). The song itself was slight, basically a harmonica-led 12-bar, with a chant-like vocal. But its vitality and infectious enthusiasm was typical of Stevie Wonder's music of the time. Gordy's packaging ideas extended to albums too. Wonder's first album, *Tribute To Uncle Ray* (1963), had been intended to capitalise on the fame of Ray Charles. In the wake of 'Fingertips', the youth aspect was played on in the title of the accompanying album, *Recorded Live – 12 Year Old Genius* (also 1963).

The success of the single made Stevie hot property, and in the next months he toured America to consolidate his position, also making his first visit to Europe. While Berry Gordy would have been happy to have Stevie continue to win over new fans on the road, the Board of Education was not. Although it had ratified his tours to date, it wanted them to be the exception rather than the rule, and requested Stevie to return to school until he graduated in 1968. Despite Gordy's fear that Stevie's career would subsequently lose its momentum (the follow-up single, 'Workout Stevie Workout', reached only Number 33), the

singer was enrolled in the Michigan School for the Blind in Lansing.

The authorities did, however, make one or two concessions; Ted Hull, a Michigan State University graduate was appointed to accompany Stevie when he was on the road in order to ensure that the young singer had four or five lessons a day. Together with producer Clarence Paul and Ardena Johnston, employed by Motown to be a mother figure for Stevie during the six months he was on the road, Ted Hull had to endure Stevie's developing sense of humour. He would deliberately walk into cars, miss a step and fall down the stairs or frighten fellow air passengers, claiming that 'This is judgement day' whenever the plane hit turbulence.

Just after Stevie commenced work on *With A Song In My Heart* (1963), his fourth album in barely five months, his voice began to break. Clarence Paul felt that the best way of helping Stevie through his voice change was to get him singing as much as possible. Ballads proved a problem, but Clarence smoothed over the cracks in Stevie's voice by singing along himself, thereby turning them into duets.

Stevie grows up

Although not a major hit, 'Castles In The Sand' continued to keep Stevie in the spotlight early in 1964; more importantly, it brought him to the attention of the Hollywood film producers. His appearances in *Muscle Beach Party* and *Bikini Beach* (both 1964) were hardly straight acting parts, but stuck in his mind as they brought him to California for the first time, 'Because . . . it is warm enough to grow oranges there and I knew those didn't grow in Detroit.'

'Hey Harmonica Man' was Wonder's only other hit single in 1964 – and the first to be issued without his diminutive prefix – but by the end of the year something far more important for his long-term career was taking place: he was beginning to write songs. Although it would be a couple of years yet before Berry Gordy would allow him to record his own numbers exclusively, there is no doubt that the early collaborations Stevie was working on with Clarence Paul, Hank Cosby and Sylvia Moy were the first fruits of a major talent. Stevie invariably came up with the tune, Sylvia did the lyrics and Hank arranged the song.

From one such afternoon's fun came 'Uptight (Everything's Alright)', the chorus of which derived from one of Wonder's favourite phrases. It reached Number 3 in the Hot Hundred and Number 14 in Britain. This UK chart debut was followed up by a short tour and a number of TV appearances. The hit single had also proved important in his homeland in winning new fans. Fan letters sent to Stevie after 'Uptight' would often be addressed simply to 'Stevie Wonder, Detroit'.

Stevie's next hit was 'Blowin' In The Wind', a Bob Dylan song that had already been a US Number 1 for Peter, Paul and

Mary in 1963, but which had been part of Stevie's live show for over a year. The version released was, in fact, a duet with Clarence Paul; it came about not only because Stevie had enjoyed singing with Clarence when his voice was breaking, but also because Stevie was in the habit of forgetting the words, and needed Clarence to prompt him. That Stevie had even got his way in having 'Blowin' In The Wind' released was remarkable enough, for Motown had hitherto steered clear of protest songs. Stevie's faith in the song was proven by its US Top Ten success.

When it became time for a new contract, Berry Gordy wasted no time in offering Wonder a further five-year pact – and, to his relief, Stevie was just as eager to continue their relationship. The year ended with *Billboard* naming him one of the top singles artists. Wonder was rapidly registering a succession of hit singles in the US charts: 'I Was Made To Love Her' (Number 2, 1967) 'Shoo-Be-Doo-Be-Doo-Da-Day' (Number 9, 1968), 'For Once In My Life' (Number 2, 1968), 'My Cherie Amour' (Number 4, 1969) and 'Yester-Me, Yester-You, Yesterday' (Number 7, 1969) all hit the Top Ten in a little over two years, while a further five singles hit the Hot Hundred.

Team work
The start of the Seventies saw Wonder in harness with some new writing partners – 'Signed, Sealed, Delivered (I'm Yours)', for example, was co-written with his mother Lula, Lee Garrett and Syreeta Wright. Lee had been a friend of Stevie's for a long time, and he, too, was black and blind. Lula was suspicious of Lee at first, as Stevie had suddenly acquired many new 'friends' and Lee's own career as a singer hadn't taken off, but he was eventually accepted.

Syreeta had recorded one unsuccessful single for Motown, and was working as a secretary at the company when Wonder got to know her and invited her along to a writing session. 'Signed, Sealed, Delivered' became one of Stevie's biggest hits, reaching Number 3 in the US and Number 15 in the UK. The same team also wrote 'It's A Shame' for the Motown (later Detroit) Spinners, notching another trans-atlantic hit as a result. That this was the result of more than a working relationship was confirmed when Stevie and Syreeta married in Detroit on 14 September 1970.

The time was fast approaching when Stevie would have to sign a new, self-negotiated contract, and Berry Gordy therefore chose to grant the singer control over his forthcoming album release. Since Stevie's previous albums hadn't sold in great quantity, there was no album-buying public to disappoint, and even if the project failed it would surely realise at least one hit single. While Stevie and Syreeta began work on *Where I'm Coming From*, Motown released Stevie's cover of the Beatles' 'We Can Work It Out' to keep his name in the public eye.

Where I'm Coming From was released on 12 April 1971, nearly one year after Stevie and Syreeta had begun writing the songs for it. Gordy got his hit single with 'If You Really Love Me', but was not over-impressed with the rest of the album, which dealt variously with ghetto life, on 'Do Yourself A Favor', and the discovery of love in the lyrical 'Something Out Of The Blue'. Not surprisingly, Stevie's view was somewhat different from that of his label: 'People are not interested in "Baby, baby" songs any more. There is more to life than that. I also think that singles are very important but I don't want to do singles only. There are some rock artists who don't want to do singles at all. I don't mind – as long as they come off an album but for me they are generally only one page in the book.'

On Stevie's reaching the age of 21, Berry Gordy and his executives praised him for all he had achieved during his ten years with the company – of the 27 singles Motown had released, eight had gone gold with US sales of one million copies and one was a platinum two-million-seller. One single had reached Number 1 in the Hot Hundred, ten had hit the Top Ten, while no fewer than 25 had figured on the *Billboard* charts. Total record sales exceeded 30 million, and Berry Gordy said he would be more than happy if Stevie would like to continue their relationship further.

All Wonder would sign, however, was a receipt for the one million dollars that the record company held in trust. Telling Motown that he wanted some time to think, he and Syreeta set up home in a New York hotel to work on the music that Stevie had wanted to do for a long time.

Freedom fighter
To handle any future business deals he appointed Johannan Vigoda, a top show-business lawyer who had previously worked with Jimi Hendrix and Richie Havens. To help him make his music, he brought in Robert Margouleff and Malcolm Cecil, electronic keyboards pioneers who had recorded as Tonto's Expanding Headband. They were to spend many hours at Electric Lady studios acquainting Wonder with the Arp and Moog synthesisers that he wanted to use on his next album. Once Stevie felt happy with what he had learned, he and Syreeta began writing the songs.

After nearly 100 songs had been recorded, Wonder was ready to talk to Motown again. The contract worked out between Stevie, Motown and Vigoda ran to a rumoured 120 pages. However, it was the content that was infinitely more important than the quantity – Stevie got the long sought-after artistic freedom to decide what tracks would go on an album, which would be released as singles, when he would go on tour, and who his support bands would be. He also formed his own publishing company, Black Bull, and production company, Taurus Productions (named after his birth sign), and his own backing group, Wonderlove.

Mind-blowing music
On 3 March 1972 Motown released *Music Of My Mind*, the album that first fulfilled Stevie's ambition to be taken seriously as an artist. In the years to come, Motown was to reap colossal reward from allowing both Stevie and Marvin Gaye the freedom to exploit the album market. (Indeed, Gaye's *What's Going On*, had just been released with scant promotion, yet was to become one of black music's biggest-selling albums.)

Music Of My Mind represented a tremendous advance on its predecessor, with breathtaking electronic keyboard textures on tracks like 'Love Having You Around' announcing that Wonder had mastered the Seventies technology he had taken such trouble to master. Sadly, its release coincided with Stevie and Syreeta's breakup, his need for a traditional marriage being at odds with her personal and musical ambitions.

By the time 1972 came, Stevie was ready to release a new album. He chose to promote the record by supporting the Rolling Stones on their mammoth US tour, and the Stones fans loved the 'new' Stevie they were hearing: *Talking Book* was to prove his finest release up to that time. It showed that Stevie's new music depended as much on white audience support as it did on his traditional black support. Wonder's image, too, was changing: gone were the jackets and crew-cut, discarded in favour of colourful African robes and beaded hairstyle.

Talking Book gave Wonder his first platinum album – and deservedly so. Jeff Beck's guitar-playing added rock credibility, while the album also included the political comment of 'Big Brother', with its lyrics clearly aimed at Richard Nixon. The album's breadth of material pleased rock and soul fans alike. The hard rhythms and funky Clavinet of 'Superstition' contrasted with the easy-listening charm of 'You Are The Sunshine Of My Life', and both songs made Number 1 in the Hot Hundred when released as singles.

Stevie's next project, for which he had set a release date of March 1973, was originally titled *Last Days Of Easter*. In his own words, it was 'about the last day of beauty. All the horror and hypocrisy in the world today. People neglecting other people's problems. And what needs doing socially, spiritually and domestically. I can only do it through my songs and I try to be positive about it.'

When the album finally appeared in August 1973, it had been re-titled *Innervisions*. Motown had previewed the album with the single 'Higher Ground', one of several tracks with a spiritual aspect. Some of Wonder's best lyrics appeared on the album, 'Visions' in particular containing visual imagery astonishing for a blind man. The album's *tour de force* was 'Living For The City', a cautionary tale of a boy from 'hard-time Mississippi' who comes to New York and is unwittingly caught up in crime and violence.

On 6 August, just three days after the

'I want to reach the people. I feel
there is so much through music that
can be said, and there's so many people
you can reach by listening to another
kind of music. That's why I hate labels
where they say "This Is Stevie Wonder
And For The Rest Of His Life He Will
Sing 'Fingertips' . . ."'
Stevie Wonder

album had been released, Stevie was a passenger in a car bound for Durham, South Carolina, when it was involved in a smash. He was rushed to hospital in a coma, remaining unconscious for some five days; many papers had already pronounced him dead, while rumour had it that, even if he survived, he had suffered lasting damage. Eventually the hospital was able to ascertain that Stevie would not suffer any permanent brain damage, and the long haul back to recovery could begin.

After two weeks in North Carolina, Motown had him moved to Los Angeles, which was considered 'closer to home', but Stevie felt alienated in LA. Still, Motown had shown good intentions, and Stevie was far more concerned with whether his musical ability had been impaired. Eventually, personal aide Ira Tucker had a Clavinet brought into Stevie's room, and it soon became apparent that all was well with the singer.

Finales and encores

Stevie made a speedy recovery from his accident, and in late September made his first public appearance on stage with Elton John during the latter's concert date in Boston. His doctors had advised against any major concerts at least until the end of the year, so Stevie was free to write songs for his next album, *Fullfillingness' First Finale*. Motown in the meantime released 'Living For The City' as a single, and it sailed into the US Top Ten.

By January 1974 Stevie had recovered enough to go back on the road. On 20 January he opened the first gala at the Midem Convention in Cannes, and then went to London to play the Rainbow Theatre. He then returned to the US to collect five Grammy awards.

At the end of March, Stevie Wonder announced that he was retiring. He intended to tour North America extensively for two years, raising money for charity, embark on a Farewell World Tour at the end of 1975, and then move to Africa to work with handicapped, blind and underprivileged children. Motown were able to convince him that he would better be able to help Africa by staying in America gaining publicity for those causes. So Stevie stayed, and in July 1974 gave Motown *Fullfillingness' First Finale* which, by the end of the year, had become his third platinum album. 'Boogie On Reggae Woman' reached Number 3 when released as a single, while the anti-Nixon sentiments of 'You Haven't Done Nothin'' took it to the top of the US charts.

While plans for an album and (abortive) world tour were mooted, Wonder cashed in

Stevie Wonder shares the spotlight with Motown chief Berry Gordy (top right), his mother and sometime co-writer Lula Hardaway (above right) and labelmate Lionel Richie (right). Left: Although better-known as a keyboardist, Stevie proved an influential drummer on his Seventies albums and, on occasion, in concert.

on past achievements by picking up another five Grammies in March 1975. A month later his girlfriend Yolanda Simmons gave birth to a baby daughter, Aisha. Stevie had met Yolanda when she had called Black Bull enquiring about a secretarial job; as Stevie was in the office he had answered the call and, liking the sound of her voice had invited her in. The birth of a son, Keita Sawandi, on 16 April 1977, confirmed Stevie and Yolanda's commitment to each other despite the shelving of marriage plans.

In spite of the signing of a seven-year contract worth 13 million dollars in August – reputedly the biggest of any recording artist – the chance of Stevie's new album, now entitled *Let's See Life The Way It Is* and scheduled as a double album, appearing that year were rapidly fading. Release dates of September 1975 and January 1976 passed and speculation mounted. All anyone now knew for certain was that the title had again changed; it would now be called *Songs In The Key Of Life*.

The collection of songs finally selected for release in early October fully merited a double album; four more were squeezed onto an accompanying EP. The highlights were many – 'Sir Duke' paid joyous homage to jazzman Duke Ellington and 'Isn't She Lovely' was dedicated to Stevie's daughter, while the haunting melody of 'Pastime Paradise' highlighted the sensitive side of Stevie's writing. *Songs In The Key Of Life*'s appearance just qualified it for inclusion in the Grammy Award nominations for that year. Some six months previously, Paul Simon had collected the Grammy Award for album of the year and had publicly thanked Stevie for not releasing an album in 1975. In 1976, Wonder was back with a vengeance; he picked up eight nominations and subsequently collected four awards which included Album of the Year.

Celluloid collaborations

The wait for Stevie's next project was to prove even longer, taking three years. Some time before the release of *Songs*, he was approached by two authors, Peter Tompkins and Christopher Bird, whose book, *The Secret Life Of Plants*, had just been published. They were working on a film version of the book, to be produced by Michael Braun, and wondered whether Wonder would be interested in scoring the music. After much thought, Stevie announced that he would begin work on it as soon as *Songs* was released.

Wonder's sightlessness meant that the very process of scoring a film was to take longer than any other project with which he had been involved. Each scene and each frame had to be carefully explained to him, while the special effects were even more complex – he taped the sounds at an airport, the sounds at a wildlife park, and the sound of waves breaking on a shore. The problematical film was never generally released, but since the project had eaten up

three years of Stevie's life, it was too late to abandon the album.

Reaction to the double LP released in October 1979 was poor. Pre-sale demand ensured that the album made Top Ten around the world, but it quickly slipped down the charts again, while three singles failed to halt the slide. Few reviewers had seen the film, and most therefore had nothing to relate the album to; nevertheless, *Journey Through The Secret Life Of Plants* undoubtedly contained some of Stevie's finest melodies.

Whatever Wonder's thoughts about his artistic credibility after *Secret Life Of Plants*, he realised that his commercial standing had taken a severe jolt, and wasted no time in launching a new album to remedy matters. It was soon evident that *Secret Life Of Plants* had had no adverse effect on his drawing power as a live performer – six nights at London's Wembley Arena in September 1980 sold out within days. Wonder chose the UK appearances to preview his new album,

Above: A friendly word of advice from Wonder to Beatle Paul McCartney in the late Sixties. The duo recorded a worldwide hit in 1982 with 'Ebony And Ivory'. Below: On stage in Paris, 1981. Opposite: Songs in the key of Stevie.

Hotter Than July, and the public acclaim that followed proved that *Secret Life Of Plants* had been no more than a slight hiccup in his career.

No fewer than four singles, each in widely differing styles, hit the UK Top Ten – a tribute to Bob Marley in 'Masterblaster (Jammin')', the country-flavoured 'I Ain't Gonna Stand For It', the classic ballad 'Lately' and 'Happy Birthday'. The last track paid tribute to the assassinated Civil Rights leader Martin Luther King, whose 15 January birthday Wonder campaigned to make a national holiday.

For his next project, Stevie felt it was time for a retrospective of his career. He had forbidden Motown to release their planned 1974 *Anthology*, but had relented three years later. *Original Musiquarium I* covered the years from 1972 to 1982, together with a side of new material. All four of the new tracks were released as singles, but *Original Musiquarium I* still sold extremely well.

In the two decades since the first Stevie Wonder record was released by Motown, he became one of the most popular musicians in the world, one of the biggest-selling recording artists and one of the biggest live attractions. Yet he has retained a characteristic humility and fellow-feeling, giving away much of the money he earns to charities. Whether or not he fulfils his 1974 ambition of working with underprivileged African children, it is certain that Stevie Wonder has enriched countless lives with his music.

GRAHAM BETTS

Black Is Beautiful

As the largest black-owned corporation in America, Motown's prestige was enormous. At a time of social and political upheaval, the company retained its unique links with the black community, dictating record tastes and fashions as well as providing a focus for material aspirations and reinforcing a positive black identity.

BLACK & PROUD

Political revolt and musical power in Sixties America

SOUL MUSIC was born out of, and became an integral part of, the social upheavals of the postwar years in the United States, when growing industrialisation led to a massive exodus of the black population from the South to the industrial cities of the North. In 1940, 77 per cent of black Americans lived in the states of the old Confederacy, but by 1960 the figure had declined to 60 per cent. And throughout the Fifties and Sixties, black Americans became politically more vociferous, pressing their claims for freedom, justice and equality.

The importance of soul music in these events stemmed from several related factors: its roots in both the rural South and the industrial North and its importance to the community, the new status black performers were beginning to enjoy as stars, and the political content, either explicit or implied, of many of the lyrics.

Soul in control

Soul was derived, through the work of pioneers like Sam Cooke and Ray Charles, from gospel and rhythm and blues. Both men had been gospel singers in their childhood and adolescence. It was Ray Charles who fused the essentially communal form of gospel with R&B, the music of the shift to the towns. And Sam Cooke was the first to develop the image of the black star – cool, feline, in control.

In the late Fifties and early Sixties an equally important role was played by James Brown. A pioneer of soul, he was born in South Carolina and brought to soul music the fervour and charisma of an evangelist preacher. By 1965, the year his immensely successful 'Papa's Got A Brand New Bag' was released, James Brown had assumed total control of both the artistic and business sides of his career, a process that paved the way for both Marvin Gaye and Stevie Wonder in the Seventies, and that provided a public example of the black artist in charge of his destiny. As his career progressed, he became more outspoken politically, both in public and in his lyrics such as 'Say It Loud, I'm Black And I'm Proud'.

The Fifties had seen a sustained assault on racial segregation in the South. The case of *Oliver Brown v The Board of Education of Topeka, Kansas* led to a Supreme Court ruling in 1954 that segregated facilities in education were 'inherently unequal'. And when, in September 1957, nine black children attempted to exercise their legal right to attend Little Rock Central High School in Arkansas, the State Governor sent 270 National Guardsmen to block their way. It was only after the intervention of the federal government, which sent 1000 paratroopers to enforce the desegregation ruling, that the children were able to continue their education.

The non-violent face of black protest, for which Martin Luther King was both a spokesman and an inspiration. His message was echoed in song by such artists as Curtis Mayfield and Marvin Gaye, thereby bringing a renewed social awareness to soul music.

In 1963 a massive campaign was launched in Birmingham, Alabama, to desegregate lunch counters and secure equal job opportunities for blacks, led by the Reverend Martin Luther King. Despite many efforts to discredit him – not least by the FBI – Martin Luther King's advocacy of non-violent direct action in the tradition of Gandhi had enormous influence.

North and South

Soul music in the Sixties came to reflect these events increasingly and was dominated by two main companies, one with its roots in the rural South and the other based in the industrial North. From 1960, Atlantic Records was closely linked (via a distribution deal) with Stax in Memphis; this powerful soul axis featured such leading artists as Joe Tex, Solomon Burke, Otis Redding, Wilson Pickett, Booker T. and the MGs, and later Sam and Dave and Aretha Franklin. With its heavy gospel leanings, the Stax/Atlantic sound was predominantly rural.

In the Northern motor city of Detroit, by contrast, Berry Gordy's Motown Corporation catered for urban sophistication with its streamlined, production line sound. The belief that racial barriers should be broken down was strongly reflected in the music of Tamla Motown. From Martha and the Vandellas' 'Dancing In The Street' (1964), written by Marvin Gaye and inspired by LeRoi Jones, the black poet and political activist, to the Diana Ross hit 'Reach Out And Touch' (1970), the Motown message was one of racial harmony.

Meanwhile in Chicago, Curtis Mayfield and the Impressions were preaching the message of Martin Luther King. Their early hit 'People Get Ready' is, at first hearing, a religious song; the train they are boarding is a gospel train. However, the general feeling the song communicates more subtly is that black people are gathering strength and moving forward to better things.

By the late Sixties, however, peaceful attempts to achieve black power seemed to be meeting with only limited success. Authorities would appear to make substantial concessions while the media spotlight dwelled upon them, but then would go only a fraction of the way when it came to picking up the cheque. In the North, whites moved out of the inner cities in droves as the blacks moved in. With them went the public services and the possibilities of loans and mortgages, leaving the centre of cities like Detroit to become a derelict wasteland.

The Black Muslim church, under the leadership of Elijah Mohammad and Malcolm X, made rapid headway in these Northern cities. They sought the establishment of a black nation-state and urged the renunciation of inherited names. Many famous black musicians and sportsmen joined the movement: Joe Tex was ordained a Muslim minister, Abdul Fakir of the Four Tops was a Muslim, as was jazz saxophonist Yusef Lateef (formerly William Evans).

There were riots in Harlem (1964), Watts in Los Angeles (1965) and Detroit and Newark, New Jersey (1967). In 1966 James Meredith went on a march in Mississippi to prove that black people there had nothing to fear – but within days he was lying in hospital, wounded by an assassin's bullet. It was on this march that Stokely Carmichael coined the phrase 'black power' – by which he meant that black Americans needed to have the power to control their own lives; without actual power they could not hope to achieve any of their goals. In the same year what was to be the most influential radical movement, the Black Panther party, was founded in Oakland, California. Members carried guns openly on the streets and shadowed police patrols to protect their own people from harassment.

The assassination of Martin Luther King in 1968 left a vacuum in the moderate black leadership, while the Panthers themselves were involved in gun battles with the FBI. A decade that opened in hope ended in near despair.

The mood of the ghetto

Soul music and black power hit the popular awareness at the same time. The 'Respect' Otis Redding wanted was from his girl – but the song also seemed a demand for greater respect for blacks in general. The Temptations under Norman Whitfield projected a tougher street-wise image and began to sing of the problems of the ghetto – from drugs and starvation to broken homes – in 'Cloud Nine' to 'Papa Was A Rolling Stone'. The death of Martin Luther King was acknowledged in the syrupy 'Abraham, Martin and John', but more significantly by Nina Simone in her moving 'Why? (The King Of Love Is Dead)', which more truthfully conveyed the black community's terrible sense of loss. Yet the following year Simone was able to transform the mood entirely with her joyful 'Young, Gifted And Black' (also recorded by Aretha Franklin), a magnificent anthem to the hopes of a new generation.

But it was Marvin Gaye who truly summed up the mood of the ghetto at the end of this turbulent decade with his 1971 LP *What's Going On*. The first record he had written and produced himself, it reflected his own struggles and sufferings as well as those of his people; his conflicts with Motown and his deep

Opposite left: Nina Simone; her 'Young, Gifted And Black' became an anthem. Opposite: A US marshal escorts James Meredith, Mississippi University's only black student, on campus in 1962. Opposite below: Black Muslim leader Malcolm X in the pulpit. Right: James Brown's songs often encapsulated the aspirations of black youth. Below: Protest on the streets, whether violent or peaceful, was frequently curbed by force.

sorrow at the death of Tammi Terrell, as well as the turmoil in America. *What's Going On* is a landmark – an important barrier in black music had been crossed, allowing it to reflect openly the political events of the time. It was impossible not to hear black America speaking, or to filter out the anguish and the pain.

DAVID MORSE

PUTTING ON THE STYLE

The ever-changing image of black stars

Top left: Seductive Sonny Til looms over his Orioles. Their visual style, however, remained impeccably smooth, as did that of fellow doowoppers the Five Willows (above left). Seventies funksters Parliament (above) provided an outrageous contrast.

WHEN THE SOUND of rock'n'roll broke out over America in the mid Fifties, it spread the phraseology, music and dress of the black ghettoes. The shock that swept the United States was largely dependent upon white youth adopting the ways of a race still considered by many white Americans to be ignorant and inferior. By defining rock 'n'roll's style – with its flamboyance, its rhythmic drive, its overt sexuality and its critical look at authority – as black style, its participants made the music an unashamedly rebel one that could not immediately be absorbed into establishment showbusiness.

The black singer's dress and his attitude in song were embodiments of the fact that his race was at odds with white authority.

The importance of the singer's image was nothing new – it had been crucial in the growth and popularity of both jazz and the blues. These genres presented two sides of life for the American black – jazz was the music of the city slicker and the ghetto sophisticate, blues that of the poor and barely literate farm or factory worker.

By the Forties, jazz was as concerned with style as it was with music. The jazz audience identified itself with the attitudes inherent in a jazzman's playing by copying his lifestyle, his clothes and habits and by talking his barely comprehensible jargon. Musicians of the calibre of Charlie Parker and Lester Young were role models for young blacks and white bohemians unwilling to support the mainstream jazz of Nat King Cole. Their style was taken up as a rejection of conventionality and the restrictions of society's rules.

Lyrics and lifestyles

Whereas the jazz image conjured up a certain amount of luxury and reflected a society that had the resources to buy clothes and drink and visit nightclubs, the blues was concerned with a presentation of self within social confines; the bluesman was inescapably part of poor society, and could only fight against it. Rather than craving the expensive lifestyle he lacked, the bluesman often concentrated his anger into the hostile shouted lyrics and the incessant rhythmic drive of the postwar urban era.

When rock came along, it took elements from both jazz and blues and welded them together with something all its own – a powerful, aggressive sexuality. The performance of the black vocal group was centred around a commitment to sensual pleasure that, to a white audience, was exotic and somewhat frightening. Black lyrics sold the promise of true love, but they were concerned rather with the white heat of passion than the rosy glow of romance. And the singers were not afraid to demonstrate it. Sonny Til of the Orioles was one of the first performers to bring explicit sexuality into his act – he moved seductively and caressed the air with his hands, so that his black audience responded with a series of ribald comments.

Clothes reinforced the idea that the singers were sexual predators. Suits were smart, shoes were sharp; the singer was smoothly groomed. Instead of neutralising the singer's potency, the well-dressed look emphasised it by contrast – and was also useful in making the black musician acceptable to whites. Chuck Berry, in the Fifties, was one such star. Immaculately

dressed in a white suit, he proceeded to taunt his audience with knowing leers, using his guitar as a blatant sexual symbol. Even in films like *Go Johnny Go!*, in which he played Uncle Tom to Alan Freed's Master, he managed to imply that he was unwilling to accept any rules other than his own.

Dance stance

The sexual innuendo that Chuck Berry had implied in the handling of his guitar was developed more explicitly in the dance routines and gymnastics used by Jackie Wilson and James Brown. Dance had always been part of a black musical act's presentation, even with vocal groups like the Cadillacs, but both Wilson and Brown used dance less as a visual entertainment than a primitive courting ritual. The sheer athleticism of their movements was wedded to a sinuous sexuality. The public image of black singers exuded confidence; in all they did, their movements, dress, their stage display, and in their lyrics, they proclaimed the message that the days of black oppression were long gone – and that, in the field of sexuality, they were masters.

Fearing that the frontiers of what a black performer could present to a white audience had been pushed too far forward, the record industry found a singer who could present a new style in a more acceptable form. Chubby Checker, unlike the athletic James Brown, was portly – cuddly rather than sexy – with an ever-ready grin that indicated friendliness and warmth, rather than rebellion. But the mainstream of black rock continued to assert its sexuality with an outrageous dress sense, symbolised by the plaid suits and ill-matching waistcoats James Brown adopted in the mid Sixties. The suit remained in vogue, but it took on an exotic character – flashy colours and shimmering fabrics glinted under the stage lights. The women used the same technique of combining the formal with the far-out, wearing cocktail dresses that would have been conventional but for their gaudy colours.

Dressed like this, artists from Motown, the biggest black-owned label, could aim at the pop market, and at white as well as black record buyers. Commercially successful singers could not rely on a style that was aimed solely at the black ghettoes, and an image had to be constructed that was true to black heritage and at the same time fitted in with white expectations and prejudices. Whereas earlier black singers could content themselves with the knowledge that their outrageous and rebellious individuality was a prime reason for their success in the white market, the Motown image had to be more universal, and therefore more respectable. For the first time, the record company it-

Reflections ... Duke Ellington (below left) and LaBelle (bottom left) brush up their images. Marvin Gaye (below) went for a more relaxed look in the Seventies, adopting the suit and sweater of the mature man of leisure.

The new clothes style was associated more with the rock community than with the black population. Sly Stone merged rhinestoned country clothing with psychedelic rock; Isaac Hayes presented himself as a sophisticated white-slave trader; and Curtis Mayfield and Marvin Gaye adopted a more casual, leatherware look – sweaters, jeans and suede jackets. Sly Stone and Isaac Hayes took fantasy roles unassociated with ghetto realities, while Gaye and Mayfield strengthened the universality of their lyrics through a visual image that was not racially specific.

From the beginnings of rock to the Eighties, the public image presented by black performers has developed from an aggressive sneer at white values into the first flowerings of a self-evaluation that no longer threatens white morality – one that stresses black pride rather than black anger. This softening is part of the greater musical and stylistic integration that has come with an increased cross-fertilisation between black and white music. PAUL FRYER

The image of Motown's stars underwent a big change in the late Sixties and early Seventies. The Temptations and Diana Ross and the Supremes (left), early subjects for Berry Gordy's grooming, had a smooth, nightclub air about them. The Jackson Five (below), no less professional, wore afros and chunky, if matching, fabrics.

self came to control the public image presented by its singers.

The rise of the Stax label in the mid Sixties coincided with the peak of two trends in black rock – on the one hand the singer as hustler, and on the other a more middle-class presentation of the black self. The first group was represented by Wilson Pickett, Joe Tex and Solomon Burke, and the second by Otis Redding, who adopted the polo-necked sweater – never a style popular in the ghettoes – and combined it with the more traditional suit to suggest a relaxed man of leisure. The adoption of white dress conventions was an aid to Redding in his move towards a white audience, and he was taken up by them as a black hero.

Shopping for clothes

New styles not associated with the ghettoes gained rapid acceptance towards the end of the decade. Whether this meant going towards African roots, or towards integrationist America, the pose of the hustler was ignored in favour of the 'natural man', a man with deep feelings about his past. The overt Africanisms in clothing and ideology were found most commonly within the jazz community, where dashikis and Afro hairstyles became the norm. In soul, the Afro was sported by artists as diverse as Aretha Franklin, Michael Jackson and Stevie Wonder. The greased, coloured and straightened hair, and the suits that had been the fashion up until the mid Sixties were rejected as copies of white fashion.

From Star to Superstar

Did Tamla-Motown start the emancipation of black musicians?

Diana Ross (below) in the film Lady Sings The Blues, *in which she plays Billie Holiday (in person, right), the great jazz singer of the Forties and Fifties. The two epitomise the changing circumstances of black singers – Holiday died in sordid circumstances after a tempestuous career, while Ross has enjoyed the enormous financial rewards of modern superstardom.*

CHESS AND TAMLA-MOTOWN have been the most important labels of Chicago and Detroit, the biggest industrial cities on the Great Lakes. Chess provided some of the most distinctive sounds in black music of the Fifties, while Tamla-Motown took over as an innovatory force in the Sixties. The rise of one and the decline of the other seem, in many ways, to symbolise changes that were gradually taking place in black music. Chess was a small label, owned by white entrepreneurs, selling rough, aggressive urban blues whose typical ambience was smoke-filled clubs. In contrast Tamla-Motown was to grow to be the largest black-owned business in the United States, and specialised in smooth, perfectly honed productions aimed at the dance floor. Furthermore,

the label had artists who could make the transition to the international concert or cabaret stage and who would demand the commensurate financial rewards.

It would not be true to say that Motown saw an enormous and immediate improvement in the status of black artists; its owner, Berry Gordy, was a businessman whose activities have been criticised, and whose associates in the cut-throat competition of American popular music have often been questionable. Tamla was the first effective record company in Detroit (even a successful white rock'n'roller like Jack Scott had to look outside the city for his recording career) and Gordy was able to snap up talent from the streets at what were very reasonable rates. He found it easy to establish a roster of talented performers relatively quickly and cheaply. But the new company was a symptom of a change; the great stars Tamla-Motown produced sustained lengthy careers at levels of financial success hitherto undreamt-of by most black stars.

Playing the percentages

There were various ways in which artists were badly treated in the Fifties. The most obvious pertained to royalties for record sales. In many instances, no royalties were paid at all; blues singers might get a flat fee of only 10 dollars for a performance, while the great Billie Holiday stated that she never received fees of more than 75 dollars per recording during the Forties.

Royalties were, in any case, absurdly low – usually one or two per cent or even less – and

The Apollo Theatre, Harlem, (top) was one of the most important venues for black artists, and featured a wide range of entertainers. Tamla-Motown stars like Gladys Knight and the Pips would inevitably head the bill in the Sixties, but in the Fifties an evening's music (above) could range from the R&B of Paul Gayten to the high-note trumpet pyrotechnics of Cat Anderson.

Art Rupe's Specialty label regularly paid a figure of only half a per cent. Compared with royalties of up to 20 per cent paid to leading groups in the Eighties, these percentages are extremely small. Thus, the rates which Motown paid in the early Sixties – 2.7 per cent to Mary Wells and 1.8 per cent to David Ruffin, for example – were not unusual and were considered quite acceptable by many.

The sums paid in royalties, or even in set fees, could be cut down in various ways. First of all, the cost of the session – the fees of session musicians, studio time, refreshments during the session (even sandwiches and beer) – were often charged to the artist. At Motown, the top session musicians earned good salaries (some up to 60,000 dollars a year in the mid Sixties) and this was paid for out of the royalties of the name artists. Royalties would also be reduced – especially in the late Fifties – by the practice of giving away free records to DJs to sell through their own shops. No royalties were paid on these copies, of course.

These methods of minimising and reducing royalties were inevitable, given that a company would want to get its hands on an acceptable product for the lowest possible cost to sell in the intensely competitive market-place of US popular entertainment. And it was also inevitable, given the number of talented musicians and singers struggling to become known, that there would be a stream of artists willing to accept these conditions, in order to make their reputation.

The market factors were, however, compounded by the failure of some companies to pay even the agreed royalties; the difficulties experienced by Del Shannon in this respect were well known. Shannon was a world-famous white singer; the problems for less successful black musicians were even worse. Through the Fifties and Sixties there was a stream of actions by artists trying to obtain their due monies – Ike and Tina Turner sued Sue Records for 330,000 dollars in the early Sixties, claiming that they'd been given false accounts. But the tangle of legal procedures (made worse in the United States by the problems of commercial legislation in different states) against corporations with experience in dealing with such matters dissuaded many singers and musicians from pursuing such a course.

Record royalties were only one difficulty, however. Publishing rights were another problem. Songwriting credits could be very lucrative, given even moderate radio airplay for a record, and held out the possibility of reaping benefits from any cover versions. Those who were aware of these possibilities were very insistent upon them. There were the celebrated cases in which Leiber and Stoller were involved: against Johnny Otis over the authorship of 'Hound Dog', and against Sam Phillips over 'Bear Cat'. But many aspiring writers or musicians felt they had no recourse but to agree to other names being added to credits, and were often willing to sell their rights for what seemed a large lump sum. Of course, whites could be exploited as well as blacks – the white Bobby Charles in New Orleans sold the rights of songs to Fats Domino – but it is undeniable that black writers tended to be worse off.

Money on stage

Given this situation over royalties and rights, the main way that an artist made money was through personal appearances. The venues where artists performed would vary. There were small local circuits for some acts; a city like Chicago had its own set of R&B clubs at which the musicians performed, and in New Orleans, venues such as the Dew Drop Inn and the Brass Rail provided regular work for local bands. There was a national circuit on which many of the R&B performers worked; juke-joints, honky-tonks and clubs throughout the South and in the black areas of Northern cities. For well-known acts audiences of between 500 and 1000 people were common – even in small Southern towns.

In the mid Fifties, top name R&B singers like Roy Brown or Charles Brown might get as much as 900 dollars per night on a tour. Lesser names might get 200 dollars. But from this fee they had to pay their expenses and those of their band. And if they weren't paid the guaranteed minimum, they had little recourse; should they cause trouble, a local redneck sheriff would have little sympathy for 'out-of-town niggers'. On some tours, singers got less than a quarter of the guarantee – and the booking agency still took its cut of that. The advent of rock'n'roll brought a national circuit of larger theatres, which package tours and the biggest stars worked in the late Fifties and early Sixties – theatres like the Apollo in Harlem, or the Regal in Chicago. And work was the operative word. Name acts such as the Coasters or the Drifters would be on the road the year round – perhaps with the Dick Clark or Irving Feld revues, or fulfilling week-long club dates. The early Motown revues undertook the same gruelling routine; some musicians were on the road 11 months per year. During one tour Martha and the Vandellas performed on 70 consecutive nights.

Managers and monopolies

Until the Motown revues of the early Sixties, most black performers of national importance were handled by a relatively small number of agencies; Universal Attractions, the Shaw Agency and Queen's Agency were particularly important, while Evelyn Johnson's Buffalo Booking Agency controlled much of the business in the South.

Some performers did well out of this system, however; the middle-rank acts at the Apollo were on 500 dollars a week in the mid Fifties. By 1960 top names – Jackie Wilson for example – might be getting 7000 dollars a week at these theatres, with a certain percentage of the gate money on top. The catch was, of course, that the artists themselves might not see anything like the amount paid for their services.

The relatively monopolistic position of the agencies, and the fact that they were often in close contact with the management of an artist meant that various undercover schemes could be worked out. Ray Charles, one of the biggest attractions of the mid Fifties, was apparently regularly cheated. His booking agents would make a spurious offer demanding 3500 dollars from a clubowner for a short residency in the club; then the real offer would be made and the club would be told they could have the singer

for 2500 dollars, plus 500 dollars in cash, which would be pocketed by the agent. The singer, only seeing the cheque for 2500 dollars, had no reason to know that he was being cheated in this way; and he also had to pay the booking agency 10 per cent of his fee (in this case 250 dollars).

Some black artists tried to fight the system, but they found it very difficult to make any headway. The tale of Roy Brown makes cautionary reading. Brown was one of the leading R&B stars of the late Forties. His first 16 singles (starting with 'Good Rockin' Tonight') all made the Top Four in the R&B charts and he and his group, the Mighty Men, won the *Metronome* award for America's most-booked group four years in a row. But Roy Brown's manager, Jack Pearl, his record company owner, Syd Nathan of King Records and his booking agent, Ben Bart of Universal Attractions, were all related, and in league with each other. And the publishing rights to the songs Brown composed were also dealt with by King Records.

Bucking the system

Gradually, during the Fifties, Brown began to realise how he was being manipulated. The trick of the double contracts – the back-hander to the booking agent – was explained to him by a member of Fats Domino's management. But Brown only saw the full extent of the deceit when BMI sent him a cheque for 1900 dollars for composer royalties on airplay of one of the cover versions of 'Good Rockin' Tonight'. King Records told him it was a mistake, but Roy had started to piece the evidence together. With the help of Dave Bartholomew, the New Orleans arranger, Brown found a lawyer; subsequent investigations revealed that BMI had been paying Brown's composer royalties to five publishing companies connected to King Records. Yet Brown himself had received nothing. In the course of this investigation, Brown also found that his record sale royalties had been consistently underpaid.

After prolonged legal wrangles, Brown was able to prove his case; the manager's licence was revoked, the agency was fined 50,000 dollars and King was banned from recording for six months. Brown then set about organising his own touring schedule. But he began to find out what it was like to buck the system. Universal Attractions still had an impressive roster of talent – including Dinah Washington, Bill Doggett and Ruth Brown – and promoters soon realised that booking Roy Brown would cut them off from these other attractions. Totally unfounded rumours were spread about the singer: that he beat his wife and children and was a liability because of dependence on drugs. Roy found that someone was booking him for two dates on the same night; he began to acquire a reputation for unreliability, for not turning up at gigs. Not surprisingly, his career suffered, even though he had ostensibly won his case.

Of course, not all black artists suffered the same fate as Roy Brown. Fats Domino has had a very successful career; partly, no doubt, because of shrewd advice from those close to him in New Orleans. Fats kept the rights to his material, and when he was signed to ABC-Paramount in 1963 he was guaranteed well over 25,000 dollars a year. He was always able to maintain his position in the business. But most black artists found it hard to exert effective pressure if they came up against crooked management, promoters who underpaid on fees or companies that cheated on royalties.

The change from Chess to Motown as a leader in black musical styles is a measure of how this situation began to change in the Sixties. Roy Brown might never have become a black superstar; but had his career peaked in the Sixties and Seventies there would have been the possibility of his making it into the big financial league, along with Motown artists like Marvin Gaye, Diana Ross and Smokey Robinson. But in the Fifties Roy Brown, popular though he was, could never aspire to that kind of wealth.   ASHLEY BROWN

Roy Brown (top left) was hugely successful in the Forties and Fifties but was denied his just rewards. Although Jackie Wilson (above) enjoyed great popularity in the early Sixties, his financial circumstances could never rival those of later stars like Marvin Gaye (top).

Epilogue

The 1970s were a period of transition for Motown. Hit by the departures of Michael Jackson, Diana Ross and Marvin Gaye, Berry Gordy appeared for a time to be unsure of the way ahead for the corporation he founded. With the coming of the 80s however, his sure touch seemed to returning, and artists such as Stevie Wonder, Gary Byrd and Rick James are carrying on the Motown tradition of developing and marketing an impressive roster of artists dedicated to producing high quality contemporary music.

MOTOWN IN THE 80s

The Detroit sound moves on

The trouble with Motown's future is that it may be overshadowed by the past. Each new hit, each new artist, may be measured by the standards of the company's peak years in the sixties. Like an Olympic athlete, Berry Gordy Jr. is in the unenviable position of trying to outperform his own record-breaking achievements.

Just a couple of years ago, he didn't even seem to be trying to do that. Diana Ross, the star most identified with Motown's growth and success, left the label when Gordy wasn't prepared to match the money she was being offered elsewhere. Marvin Gaye, one of two performers hailed for helping 'Hitsville USA' adjust to the album-oriented seventies, also quit amid charges of creative interference and career insensitivity. And Jobete Music, Motown's immensely profitable publishing division, was very nearly sold.

But 1983 apparently marked a change in Berry's attitude towards the $100 million enterprise he built from an $800 family loan. The year was proclaimed as the company's 25th anniversary and much energy and money poured into the creation of a star-studded television special to celebrate that anniversary. When nationally broadcast by NBC-TV on May 16, 1983, 'Motown 25: Yesterday, Today, Forever' was a bona fide smash. Close to 50 million Americans tuned in, to make it the highest-rated show of the week. The programme subsequently won an Emmy award, television's equivalent of Hollywood's Oscar.

The real triumph of 'Motown 25' was the fact that Berry Gordy secured the participation of so many of his former artists: Ross, Gaye, the Jacksons, the Four Tops, Martha Reeves, Mary Wells, Jr. Walker. They performed with enthusiasm and goodwill alongside such stalwarts as Stevie Wonder, Smokey Robinson and the Temptations, and were happy to acknowledge their tremendous debt to Motown, no matter the manner of their parting.

An emotional affair, the show intensified Gordy's renewed interest in the music business. He became personally involved in negotiations for the company's product to be distributed by MCA Records, after 25 years in the hands of independent distributors. The move, though highly criticized by those same distributors, was seen as improving Motown's sales and profits in an increasingly competitive US marketplace.

On the creative side, Motown re-signed the Four Tops and Jr. Walker, and em-

Gary Byrd (right) is one of the most successful young talents to be developed under Stevie Wonder's Wondirection label.

company can no longer be the paternal organization it once was, by law and by location (Los Angeles has more lawyers per square foot than Detroit did). Berry Gordy acknowledged the change: 'I don't think economics would ever let it be like it was with us again. We had a whole artist development department, and everyone had to go through that department. But now that everyone not only has a mind of their own, but also an attorney's mind and an agent's mind, it's not the same atmosphere, because it's more money-motivated'.

The contemporary Motown roster combines familiar names and fresh faces. Smokey Robinson still makes mellifluous music, even as his Sixties classics are regularly remade by other pop and R&B acts. Stevie Wonder remains an innovative force not only through his own recordings, but also by the development of new talent – most recently, Gary ('The Crown') Byrd – on Wondirection Records.

In addition to the newly returned Four Tops and Jr. Walker, other fixtures include the Temptations (associated with Motown for more than 20 years, aside from a brief spell with Atlantic Records), Syreeta (15 years) and the Commodores/Lionel Richie (12 years).

Among the label's newer acts, the most popular is Rick James. Since 1978, this self-assured native of Buffalo, New York, has been responsible for album sales exceeding 10 million – including his own hits such as *Come Get It, Street Songs* and *Cold Blooded*, and those he's produced for Teena Marie, the Stone City Band and, more recently, the Mary Jane Girls.

Strictly speaking, James' Motown connection stretches back to the late Sixties. He was then a member of the Mynah Birds (supposedly contracted to the label, although no product was released) and a composer with the name Ricky Matthews, whose songs 'Malinda' and 'Out In The Country' were recorded by Bobby Taylor on Gordy Records.

Almost 10 years later, Gordy was the imprint under which Rick's 'You And I' single and *Come Get It* LP appeared, both major 1978 hits and the beginning of his golden streak as a singer, songwriter and producer.

The DeBarge family from Grand Rapids, Michigan, has produced a couple of Motown's newer attractions. Brothers Tommy and Bobby DeBarge were founder members of Switch, who collected R&B chart entries with 'There'll Never Be' and 'I Call Your Name' before departing for another record company. The more lasting property has been DeBarge, the quintet comprising brothers Bunny, Randy, Mark and James, and sister Eldra. Their 1983 hits 'All This Love' and 'Time Will Reveal' were melodic, harmony-filled singles in tune with America's burgeoning AC (Adult Contemporary) radio format.

Motown has also done relatively well with Michael Lovesmith, the Dazz Band, Bobby Nunn and Finis Henderson, among

barked upon new relationships with some old associates: Norman Whitfield and Holland/Dozier/Holland. Whitfield worked with Walker and the Temptations, while the H/D/H team produced the Tops. Asked about the bitterness and lawsuits which originally separated Motown and its most successful creative team, Eddie Holland said, 'That was so long ago we can't even remember what started it'.

Similar sentiments were expressed by other ex-Motowners, bathing in the glow of the 25th anniversary festivities. 'Motown was the best thing that ever happened to us', said Martha Reeves, in contrast to the sharp words she had after leaving the label years ago. Talking about record royalties

As well as providing the founder members of Switch, the talented Debarge family also produced the successful quartet (top) that bears its name. The sparkling Dazz Band (above) carry Motown's tradition of slick staging and polished professionalism into the eighties. Far right: A newer Gordy star, Rick James, has links with Motown that hark back to the sixties.

that she and others might have been due at the time, Mary Wells stated, 'They invested in clothes, musicians, recording. We didn't feel abused'.

Motown's investment in artists continues in the eighties, of course, although it's a very different record business. The

others. Lovesmith, known for session work and, in the early Seventies, an affiliation with Holland/Dozier/Holland's Invictus and Music Merchant labels, has delivered a couple of highly commendable albums, *Lovesmith* and *I Can Make It Happen.* The Dazz Band laboured first as Telephunk, then as Kinsman Dazz, before hooking up with Motown and producer Reggie Andrews to record 'Let It Whip', a pop and R&B smash in 1982.

An Earth, Wind & Fire connection unites Bobby Nunn and Finis Henderson. Philip Bailey produced the former when part of an act named Splendor, while Al McKay produced the latter after he left Chicago's Weapons Of Peace for a solo career. First Motown hit for Henderson was 'Skip To My Lou' in 1983; Nunn charted with 'She's Just A Groupie' the year before.

Motown continues to show an inclination to record music other than contemporary R&B. Berry Gordy signed Jose Feliciano as part of an attempt to reach the Latin market, and released his updates of such Detroit oldies as 'Lonely Teardrops' and 'I Second That Emotion'. Morocco (*Motown Rock Company*) was launched as a modern version of the Rare Earth label, and debuted with a movie soundtrack, *Get Crazy.*

In fact, soundtrack packages *(The Big Chill, Christine)* seem to be the only reminder of Berry's once-torrid love affair with Hollywood. The company hasn't bankrolled any major motion pictures since *The Wiz*, a box-office disaster, and the absence of Diana Ross now clearly limits the firm's future film opportunities.

Home video is another matter. A version of the 'Motown 25' TV show is being released for the home market, reportedly with an extra 20 minutes of footage not seen in the original. Gordy would be foolish, too, if he didn't explore the commercial appeal of video compilations featuring the 'Hitsville' stars of yesteryear. Imagine a video equivalent of the Supremes' or the Temptations' greatest hits, drawn from their TV and stage appearances of the sixties. The label is thought to own rights to a substantial amount of this type of material.

But to future generations of music fans, it'll be names like Richie, James, DeBarge, Nunn and Lovesmith – or perhaps others, yet undiscovered – that will be as important as Ross, Gaye and Robinson were before them. Chances are, one of Motown's competitors during the next 25 years will echo the words of one of the company's competitors during the past 25, Ahmet Ertegun. 'They make the records they know how to make', the Atlantic Records chief said, 'and they still make them better than anybody else'.
ADAM WHITE